DC

WISHING YOU WERE FISHING!

A GUIDE TO HELP YOU CATCH MORE FISH

By Professional Fishing Guide and Tournament Bass Angler

Daniel H. Sturges

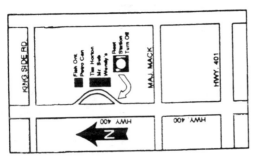

PREFACE

Wishing you were Fishing is a practical guidebook. The author has nearly a half century of Ontario game fishing experience. He is an active Pro Bass competitor and has shared the podium with some of Ontario's finest anglers. In the last several years he has been given the privilege to be a guest host consistently on The Ultimate Fishing Show.

This book is about giving its readers the advantage of experience. That advantage is a fishing savvy that describes where, when and how to fish fresh water game fish species using live and artificial baits and conservationists catch and release techniques. Don't get me wrong! This book is not just about savvy and technique in Ontario. It calls upon its readers across North America to go back to their favorite fishing haunts and try again by utilizing some of their new found knowledge. The proof is in the "poonas" (fish in foil or clay baked under a campfire).

Wishing you were Fishing will guide its readers to maximize their major definite purpose of selecting and using the right bait presentations and techniques to land the big one that otherwise might have never even got to taste your hook. Simply, it should help you catch more fish!

ABOUT THE AUTHOR by Douglas Sturges (brother)

I remember our first fishing experience as brothers. We were fishing beneath the old iron bridge on Islington Avenue near Albion Road in what is now known as Etobicoke, very near Toronto. All five brothers and our Father were fishing for shiners using bamboo poles. Even on this fishing trip our first adventure together, Dan caught the biggest fish.

After our move up Islington Avenue to the village of Woodbridge we frequently continued our family tradition. Soon after our move *Hurricane Hazel* arrived and reshaped the Humber River banks and to some extent purified it.

I remember one day, to our father's horror, the chief of police Herb Weatherall, showed up at our house with the author in tow (1956). He had found the five year old alone under the bailey bridge fishing rock bass amid the new rock formation left by *Hurricane Hazel.* Daniel (Boone) as we called him then, was clear that the spoils of the flood had created new structures making his spot even better as a fishing location.

During his later childhood my brother Dan continued to fish that local river inventing techniques like placing a red button above a split shot to jig for rock bass with a made to measure hockey stick as his rod. I vividly remember him coming home with a monster Rock bass, it had to have been over five pounds and had we known then it could have made the record books.

Dan has since landed many trophy fish and catches them on his own lures. Some of his trophy catches include a couple of Walleye over nine pounds caught in land locked lakes in the Haliburton Highlands where he has been guiding for the past ten years, several speckled trout over five pounds and a King salmon just over thirty-two pounds. I leave those stories to the author and the pages of his book. Its worth noting his first Pro Tournament ranked him and his partner Paul Terhart in the top ten. To their delight they ranked well above some of the popular big named anglers.

PROFILE OF THE AUTHOR

Daniel Sturges has spent more than "four decades" successfully fishing the many pristine lakes throughout South/Central Ontario and including the Great Lakes in search of the many species of game fish available to an enthusiastic angling specialist. Concentrating for the last ten years on the Kawartha Lakes and the Haliburton Highlands area as a professional fishing guide. In the last several years he has dedicated a lot of his time competing in the prestigious Chevy Truck/Mariner Marine Pro Bass Tour sharing the waters with Rocky Crawford, Les

Zachny, Bob and Wayne Izumi, Wes Lavergne and Erny Janzen. Dan has been featured as guest host every year since 96 on the popular Ultimate Fishing Show. This particular show focuses on teaching anglers methods to improve their fishing skill level by demonstrating techniques and tips from a select group of Professional Anglers.

At a very young age you could find Dan fishing regularly with his four older brothers, his Father and many times with their Grandfather. Coming from a large family, a tree branch, a hook, line, sinker and bobber concluded his tackle selection. Quickly his passion for this sport developed into a relentless obsession in pursuit of trophy Game fish. Eventually he became a progressive angler, sporting a number of specialty rods during each outing.

For him the excitement started in May each year and continued until the lakes froze, then ice fishing began, until mid-March. Between March and April he would be in attendance at fishing shows sharing his vast knowledge as a fishing product consultant.

This is Dan's first book on his favorite subject although it may not be his last. If it sells well he plans to write a Guidebook for youngsters six to sixteen. His theory is, his best fishing teacher was himself and only wishes that someone had thought of writing a guide book for youngsters sooner!

IN APPRECIATION

Without these friends and family members, I couldn't have completed this book. Tracy Maynard, Audrey Donnelly, Ron MacRae, George Gouvianakis, 'HOT ROD SCOTT' Anderson, Lorrie McCauley, Paul Dryer, Chris Stasoff, Scott Martin, Jim Sturges Sr., Jim Sturges Jr., Vaughan Fire & Rescue "A" Platoon 73.

The continuous support from my beautiful wife Diane and my three wonderful children and "Fishing Buddies", Matt, Phil and Eric who continue to make me a proud father!

I must also mention that, if it wasn't for Joe Coniglio the publisher and a great friend, this fishing book would have never transpired. Thank You all!

Cartoonist Paul Davies drew each of my fishing cartoons. Great Job Paul!

Artist Cory Trepanier for taking time out of his fine art studio to design the book cover. Fabulous job!

TO THE READER

First and foremost I would like to thank you for purchasing your copy of "Wishing you were Fishing" and I trust it has or will benefit you on your next several fishing trips. For me, fishing is only as difficult as one makes it, although the more I learned the simpler it became. The goal I am trying to reach in compiling this book was to make it easier for anyone that showed an interest. The essential choices of equipment and effective angling practices are equally as important.

Finding time in our busy daily schedule and being able to have the cooperation of family and friends to join us in our quest for hunting that monster fish that doesn't manage to get away. Life is too short! So take hold of the reins and take charge or organizing that long over due fishing adventure before you find yourself scratching your head and mumbling. "I wish I had done this sooner!"

After reading this book, I would like to share with you a couple of familiar words.

GO FISH!

The Fishing News

table of contents

CHAPTER THREE · Trout Tactics 90

CHAPTER ONE
Fishing Fundamentals

FISHINARY DEFINITIONS (FISHING TERMS)

This information has been installed at the front of the book to assist many of the readers in comprehending unfamiliar terms and descriptions.

LURES USED IN THIS BOOK

Top Water: These types of bait presentations are designed to be effective in water as little as two to approximately eight feet in depth, or within view of an ambushing fish's strike zone. Described as a "sitting duck" provoking presentation! ie: Zara-Spook, Skidder Pop, Torpedo, Spittin' Image, Snagproof, Frog or Mouse.

Shallow, Sub-surface crank baits have a small front bill which is designed to make it run from six inches to as much as two feet. The idea of these baits is to trick any fish searching for surface food in water about four to twelve feet in depth ie: Rapala Originals, Long A's, Bomber Shads or Smithwicks.

Deep Divers: Easily identified by the spoon billed front lip, these baits are designed to run at approximately eight to fifteen feet in depth. They perform best in water depths of eight to twenty-two feet, determined by your retrieval speed ie: Rattle Traps, Rapala's Fat Raps, Shad Raps and the Risto Raps.

Suspending: Specifically designed to imitate an injured or dying bait fish (minnow). Built with a special technological feature known as "neutral buoyancy". This allows the bait to sink to a specific depth and no further (approximately three feet). This style of bait performs best in depths of four to eighteen feet. Look for the word "suspending" when purchasing some. ie; Pradco's, Rattlin' Rouge or Mystic's and Rapala's Husky Jerks.

Jerk Baits: These baits were designed for primarily predator fish such as the Northern pike and Muskies. These baits are designed to imitate injured or dying bait fish. A cast, pause, twitch and pause, jerk retrieve, using a long stiff rod to create splashing sound each time you torpedo the bait towards you. Heavier fishing lines are highly recommended, at least 20# test or even better, braided line. Smithwick's, Believer, Leo Lures and the Rapala's Husky Jerks are very good choices.

NATURAL BAITS (Live)

Dew Worms: Are by far the most popular choice. Because of their availability and probably anyone who has ever tried fishing, started with worms. Worms can catch almost every species of freshwater fish that can fit one in their mouth.

Earthworms: Best for panfish such as perch, sunfish, crappie and rock bass. Use of a small hook is suggested. Works quite well on all species of gamefish, although they will only catch small Northern pike and musky.

Minnows: You can catch every variety of fresh water fish using minnows: creek chub, dace, suckers or emerald shiners are your choices. When fishing for northern pike or musky use shiners or suckers in 5" to 9" range. Rule of thumb: smaller bait for smaller mouthed fish.

Leeches: Found in most fresh waters lakes, emerge from sand bottom as lakes warm in early spring.A popular alterative for ardent bass and walleye fishers who generally consider worms.

Crayfish: Work very well on bass, walleye and the occasional rainbow trout provided you rig with a standard bait hook (no sinkers), tied direct and let the crayfish descend on it own although you will have to lift it up before it makes it to the bottom. By doing this you will be presenting it naturally.

Frogs: Although frog season is a little shorter than the rest of the live baits, they are preferred by big bass if you can place them in their strike zone accurately.

Book Worm: : At least half of my fishing knowledge was found in either a book, magazine or brochures. When in "doubt" sign a book out "Knowledge is Power"!

WISE BAIT CHOICES

Whenever you are ready to venture out to visit your favourite fishing hole, be sure you know what the fish habitually prefer to feed on. By gaining this important knowledge, your bait selections can be reduced by as much as fifty percent.

Gamefish generally feed on emerging (hatching) aquatic life, ie. leeches, crayfish and insect nymphs. This occurs annually during the spring and continues throughout the opening of trout, northern pike and walleye season. In the case of trout, you will have to include spawn or roe (trout and salmon eggs) with your bait choices. These species also dine on a variety of bait fish (minnow sized) as well as occasionally turning to take their young (cannibalistic).

Your options are to stick with artificial only or pick your own dew worms or buy live bait at a bait place on your way. Traditionally, a majority of Ontario angler's choose live bait, with dew worms being their first choice. Imitation baits that most resemble live baits are as follows:

Leeches: Berkley's Power leeches in black motor oil, and dark coloured power grubs standard size and micro-sized.

Crayfish: Berkley's Power tube bodies in blue fleck, como fleck and pumpkin seed, made ready by inserting a tube jig (lead) weighted hook into the tube body.

Nymphs: Berkley's Power grub bodies in assorted earth tone colours, made ready by inserting the body over a coloured jig head that matches in colour.

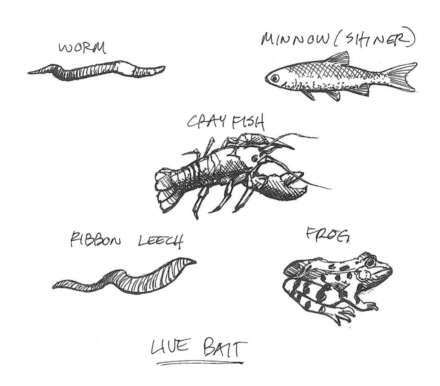

WORM

MINNOW (SHINER)

CRAY FISH

RIBBON LEECH

FROG

LIVE BAIT

Minnows: Berkley's Power shads in red, smoke and silver on a black body, installing them on dark coloured "painted" jig heads. The most popular jig head weight is 1/4 & 1/8 oz. for most Power Baits.

These baits are probably the best on the market because they are scent impregnated and out perform plastic. The key is to try to make them move naturally by "finessing" them during your retrieve. An important point that might be overlooked is, that when the word emerging is mentioned, you must present your bait, just up from or on the bottom to increase your percentages of strikes.

As the lakes warm up, you will be safe to switch your baits to primarily minnow imitations such as crankbaits, ie. Wally Divers, Yo-Zuri's, Smithwick's Rattlin' Rouge or Rapala's Husky Jerks and Shad or Fat Raps to coax the toothy characters.

You will find that by mimicking baits that are indigenous to your lakes, you will have constant producers. Examples: Minnows in perch, shad, shiner or sucker colours. Crayfish in tube jigs or crayfish in plastic or pork in earthtone colours. Leeches, black grubs or leech shapes will always work.

I don't recommend using artificial worms when fishing for any species of trout because they are designed primarily for bass. Also, when fishing for speckled trout, you will increase your catch and reduce injuring them by reducing your hook size and switching to ultra-lite tackle. The average size of speckled trout is about ten inches. Tiny fish, tiny hooks!

NATURAL WORM PRESENTATION (Walleye)

As a youngster, I was taught how to pull my own dew worms to satisfy my ever growing need for fresh bait. During this time I practiced gobbing them on as many times as it took to conceal the hook. For some unknown reason, I felt there had to be a better way to increase the effectiveness although this method always produced lots of fish; I was trying to catch the biggest fish.

Several years later I discovered a fishing show that constantly introduced new methods on almost every show. This method involved worms only. It implied that it would work on all species of game fish. After using this method for over ten years, the opportunity arose where I could pass the information on to other anglers. I felt with the book coming up it wouldn't be complete if I neglected to mention it also.

Using a conventional two piece spinning rod and reel spooled with your favourite mono or copolymer 6 or 8# test clear fishing line. Rig it with a Lindy walking sinker 1/4 oz., followed by a single Water Gremlin split-shot (weight) size BB. To complete this rig, tie on a Gamakatsu or Eagle Claw "bait holder" hook. To install your worm, count back from the nose (dark end) five rings, then pierce the hook through both sides of the worm and you're ready. To effectively present this rig you have to follow the instructions to the letter:

1) Position your boat parallel to the breeze and make a gentle lob cast into the wind, allowing the line to run free until it touches bottom.

2) Leaving your bail open, control the line using the pad of your index finger.

3) Drifting at wind speed only, drop your fishing line as soon as you detect a tap, let the fish run with it for ten seconds if it was an aggressive bite, fifteen seconds if it was taken lightly.

4) Close your bail by tripping it with the reel handle, wait for your line to straighten, then sweep set the hook.

5) Play the fish to the side of the boat and have the net person stand by until you give the okay! Net it head first.

There are several alternatives for this presentation, you can replace the hook with a #2 floating jig head and you do everything exactly the same, on a day where there is hardly a breeze or you can inject your worm using a worm blower. This prevents the bait from sinking where it could disappear into the bottom silt.

This method is as effective when using leeches or small minnows. To reduce the risk of line twists you may exchange the split shot with a crane swivel. By following these simple steps, you will catch at least twice as many fish as have in the past. Using a fish finder (sonar) to locate your fish can save you countless hours of fishing dead space. You will however, use twice as many worms to catch twice as many fish.

TERMINOLOGIES

Strike Zone: Fish are not equipped with peripheral vision. Because of the position of their eyes on their heads, plus the fact they have no eyelids. This restricts their vision to straight ahead or just above their nose and out to the sides. Hence their "Strike Zone". These distances will vary generally, dictated by the amount of light penetration and water clarity.

Structure: Half the battle is realizing most game fish thrive in and around underwater structure. Anything other than a sand bottom can be classed as structure. Smaller fish try to take cover in structure, which in turn draws feeding fish to these areas, ie. boulders, drop offs, edges, humps, weeds, tree falls, islands, docks, boat houses, and rock piles are just a few.

Ideal Conditions: During a full or new moon phase with normal seasonal temperature for three days, slightly over cast, gentle breeze coming from the west or south. No apparent fishing pressure for at least a week. Presentations should replicate forage indigenous to that specific body of water ie; Minnows, Crayfish or Leeches. Fish methodically in probability areas exercising caution during a take. Monitor your rod tip and the line direction to ensure your best hook-set.

TROLLING METHODS

Straight: Straight behind, your boat port side or starboard side, (flat line), no down rigger. Using lures at no fixed depth. Lighter lines will run deeper than greater pound tests, less resistance.

Down rigging: Behind a boat utilizing down rigger equipment to maintain fixed depths. With two or more riggers consider placing the rods away from one another to avoid entanglement. Cannon balls or down rigger weights are available in different weights and shapes for improving presentations. We call this "fixed depth" fishing trolling.

Side Planer: Generally used by walleye anglers and sometimes by charter boat captains for spring rainbow trout. The implementation of additional rigging and equipment to present an artificial bait (lures)away from engine noise.

Back Trolling: Wise anglers use this method on days when there isn't enough of a breeze to drift. By comparison, back trolling is a little slower because you troll in reverse which uses your transom (back of the boat) to reduce your trolling speed.

Vadeling (Zig-Zag): By using this technique you will become more successful because you are changing the speed of your lures constantly each time turn to change direction, also you will cover far more water.

Drifting: Using the speed of the breeze to allow your presentation to come into sight at the most natural speed. You can virtually cover twice as much area of a lake. Probably the most productive live bait method. Preferred by many Walleye anglers.

Trolling in 'Prop-wash': Using larger minnow imitations you can make these baits look like an injured or dying bait fish. A Musky and Northern Pike technique. The fish don't hit your lure, they attack it.

TYPES OF FISHING LINES

Monofilament: Single (mono) clear or coloured, a general purpose fishing line, probably the most popular and widely used. This is available in 4#-30# test with different properties such as memory, stretches and develop weaknesses through abrasion and the ultra violet rays. Should be changed at least a couple of times per season to avoid disappointments.

Copolymer: A cored polymer line or a line within a line. This line has advanced technological properties, which include microscopic diameters, reduced abrasion, low stretch, virtually no memory (can be stretched, will return to its original shape) and it has an improved wet knot strength. All these properties are related to its high performance levels. Available in 4# - 30 pound test.

Braided: A microscopic synthetic rope. Its special fibres (Spectra) gives it about five times the strength of equal diameter line. More durable than both monofilament and copolymer lines and does not

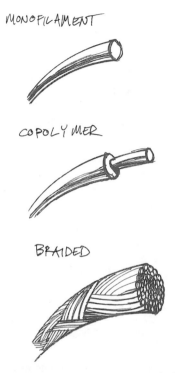

MONOFILAMENT

COPOLYMER

BRAIDED

have to be changed as often. Highly recommended for increased angler control when fishing heavy cover for bigger species of game fish. Available 5# to 80# test.

Fluorocarbon Line: One of our newest lines making waves in the fishing industry is 100% fluorocarbon. In the past this line has become the first choice of experienced Float and Fly fishers as their preferred leader lines. It has an outstanding property, it's virtually invisible in water. This gives your bait offerings the look of the most natural presentation. Even the fish think there are no strings attached. Easy to cast, invisible and great knot strength!

CHOICES OF FISHING RODS

As a novice angler, a spin-caster is probably a popular choice, although, by ten years old you should wean your youngster off this type of rod and introduce them to a medium priced "spinning outfit". Simplicity is important when you are first introduced to fishing, unfortunately you could find it difficult to make the transition to this new style of fishing. Your reel operates on top of a spin-cast rod, while the reel is operated from under a spinning outfit. A spinning rod and reel combo will make live bait presentations your easiest choice when pursuing most game fish species.

As you progress your desires will sway you toward advancing to using a baitcaster and trigger rod. This will allow you to become extremely versatile when using a wide variety of artificial bait presentations.

BAIT CASTING ROD Primary use is for casting artificial lures and sometimes trolling (flat lining). Average length is 7' (one piece). Also available in 6'6", 7'6" and 8' lengths.

PISTOL GRIP Similar to baitcast although designed for lighter duty. Average lengths. A single handed rod using mainly your wrist and forearms.

CASTING ROD Initially designed for casting and trolling for Pike and Musky.

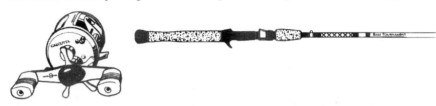

FLIPPIN' ROD A stiffer and longer rod designed to 'horse' big bass out of weedy areas using finesse baits. Common length 7' to 8'. Available in telescopic style.

DOWNRIGGER ROD Specifically designed for fixed depth fishing using a downrigger for trolling. Usually 7' to 8'6" in length and constructed using fiberglass blanks for better upright pull when fishing for Salmon and Trout.

Fishing Fact: Why use "salted" baits? When a fish strikes and tastes salt, it implies injury (blood tastes salty). Because the fish holds on tighter you will improve the percentages of a better hook set.

FLY ROD Completely different design for fly presentations, best described as a gentle application. Commonly available in line weights 5 to 9 weights.

SPINCAST Primarily used to introduce fishing to youngsters. Used for panfish, ie: perch, crappie, catfish, sunfish and rock bass. Mainly live bait presentations. Line weights #8, or #10 test.

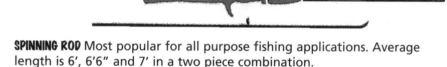

SPINNING ROD Most popular for all purpose fishing applications. Average length is 6', 6'6" and 7' in a two piece combination.

TRIGGER ROD (long-pole) Primary use is casting for bass by flippin', pitchin', finessing or rip jigging. Can also be used when fishing Pike or Musky. Preferred lengths 5'9" to 8' long.

Although a variety of specialty rods can make you more versatile, it probably will take lots of practice to be both comfortable with this new equipment and as much time to become proficient with the new presentations.

Remember, your best lure is your confidence level and of course "knowledge is power".

HELPFUL HINTS FOR FILLING YOUR REELS

Spinning Reels: To get your fishing reel to operate at its optimum, simply read the suggested ratings on the reel spool.

Generally most spinning reels recommend from 4# test to 10# test, monofilament or copolymer. Braided can be spooled on provided they don't exceed the rated pound test.

Spooling Line: The trick when spooling your reel properly is, be sure that you first observe which way the line arcs, it must be installed so the arc wraps on the reel the same way. Otherwise you will have your line coming off on its own and create all kinds of casting problems.

Note: Personally, I don't recommend using "super lines" on spinning equipment" unless you use extreme caution in selecting small diameters. Names to look for are *Spiderwire, Raptor* and my favourite, *Power Pro.*

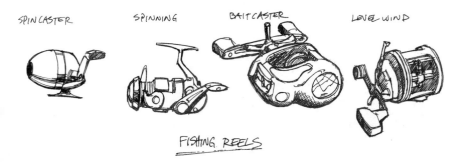

SPIN CASTER   SPINNING   BAITCASTER   LEVEL WIND

FISHING REELS

'CO-ORDINATED' FISHING

You can sometimes tell an angler's skill level by their selective choices of equipment and lures. To select equipment for specific species can sometimes be difficult. One of the necessary components for being a successful angler is having the knowledge of game fish habitat; daily feeding habits, influences by changing weather conditions and seasonal movements, which generally dictate their food sources.

Game fish have different scheduled spawning times previous to the season openers. By picking up a copy of your fishing regulations you can be informed of the exact days. Depending on your fishing locations most seasons opening day falls on or very near the same day.

There are many categories and types of anglers such as, dock and shoreline fishers, weekend and occasional fishers, avid and obsessed anglers and fly fishers. I may have missed a few, although you have the idea.

If you are an occasional angler, you will most likely be using a rod and reel combination suited for general purposes. This would mean that basically you would fish for bass or maybe walleye during the summer months on days of fair weather. On a rainy or windy day, I'll bet you will participate in your three meals a day. On other days, you can be found, wishing you were fishing! The thought of putting on a rain coat and heading out to fish probably would never cross your mind.

For a little more devoted angler, you might find them sporting a better quality rod and reel combination, a more select variation of lures, and storing it in a higher capacity tackle box.

If your equipment doesn't last much more than a year then it's time to upgrade. You won't ever regret fishing with premium equipment as it will improve your self-confidence as well as reduce the number of fish lost by mechanical failure.

Although many people may argue this fact, they won't have information to back it up.

Most progressing angler situations tend to develop a more serious approach by improving their daily catch. People seem to concentrate more towards one species of fish rather than make it become a personal challenge.

As an example, if bass is your preferred choice, then the purchase of a second rod would be eminent. The new rod would most likely be a bait caster, if you plan to progress. Although the transition may take you back in confidence, regular practice can benefit you indefinitely.

In talking to many fellow anglers, I found some admitted they could not deal with it due to the different style of presentations. For others who managed to adjust to the new equipment quickly, they began talking of additional rods to become even more versatile.

Like anything new, it will take time to become proficient with it. When buying more selective equipment you can eliminate most of the frustration by dealing with experience. Find a local store that specializes in fishing equipment and can refer you to the nearest warranty and repair place. I call this shopping with confidence!

TACKLE STORAGE SYSTEMS

When it comes to purchasing a new tackle box, there are a number of things to consider. Your old tackle box may have become obsolete if its lasted longer than five years. Keeping in mind that if you want your new one to last much longer, you might decide on spending a little more to get your moneys worth.

I purchased a conventional tackle box (container) assuming it was going to serve me well. Although after tripping over it several times in a day and having to spend valuable fishing time reorganizing it, I realized it was not meeting my expectations.

As my tackle supply increased, I moved to a Lid Locker that I hoped would be ideal —I could arrange the tackle to suit my immediate needs by loading the top transparent tray. One day, after a great day of fishing, I was walking on a dock loaded down with several rods, a portable fish finder, my net, some P. F. D.'s (personal flotation devices) and this fantastic tackle box, I almost made it to shore. The plastic front closure snapped and every single piece of tackle spewed out. Some on the dock, but most of it plopped into a shallow weedy area of the lake. I was not amused; all I could see was red!

After about two weeks of spousal therapy, I ventured out to buy a double sided satchel. It was important by this time to get a more compact style box with a good capacity to house my array of ever improving tackle.

This time I felt very confident that it was going to be a hazard-free box. It took all my tackle, except my fish scents and about two handfuls of grubs and twister tails. By now you can imagine that I am somewhat of a impulse buyer, when it comes to tackle.

So to remedy this problem, it was time for a serious purchase, a soft storage tackle system. Although they are a little pricey you can co-

Fishin' Georgian Bay near Owen Sound, Ontario
...Slamin' Salmon.

ordinate everything and put them in separate translucent stackable boxes with room to spare. Even if you dropped it overboard, you wouldn't spill anything and besides it floats. The individual boxes load into a lightweight zippered bag and can be carried over your shoulder or in one hand. You can also buy extra stackables and mark each one for specialized fishing.

For years I have been habitually cloth bagging my rods and transporting them in plastic tubes to protect them from damage. My reels go in a small tackle box that I've lined with foam underlay to protect them from accidentally being damaged during transport. With the new tackle system I am able to transport everything with complete confidence that it will arrive intact and no worse for wear. Some brand names to look for are Plano, Flambeau's (soft tackle systems), and Pinnacle. They are all very well designed. No matter what type of fishing you do, the soft tackle systems are becoming angler's first choice.

LURE MODIFICATION

You must be cautious when modifying store bought fishing tackle. Although most of your new tackle will have been tested and recommended by a large group of successful Pro tournament angler's from the USA. With the fact that these baits were tested in American waters, does not mean they will perform as well up here in our lakes. Some examples of modified baits:

- SUSPENDING BAIT
- SCENTING BAITS
- ADDING PRISM
- AFFIXING PROMINENT EYES
- RUBBER CORE WEIGHTS
- HOOK CHANGES
- SPOON BILL ADJUSTMENTS
- SPLIT RINGS

SUSPENDING BAITS

Have you ever wondered what happens to your worm or leech when you cast it out allowing it to sink to the bottom? Probably it becomes lost in the silt or weeds. By using a floating jig head or injecting the worm creating a 1/4" bubble, your bait is put right in front of the fish's nose. This is called putting it in the strike zone.

SCENTING BAIT

A little trick I practice is, the evening before a fishing trip I select a number of jelly baits such as grubs, worms, and lizards. Separate each by placing them in sandwich bags (zip-lock), then pour about a teaspoon of appropriate scents into each bag. My bait is now scented for tomorrow's fishing. You can keep it in the scent for about a month or longer. If you need to add more scent you can. —Similar to the above mentioned trick, you can do the same with your pork rinds by dumping out the brine and replacing it with a suitable scent. Because the rind is already saturated with brine water it's advisable to allow it to sit in the fish scent for at least three days. When the rinds are all used up, save it for the new jar. You can squeeze the moisture out of the pork pieces and then drop them in the scent.

ADDING PRISMS

On a select number of lures you can add a coloured prism tape to stimulate a strike. One that is commonly improved is for salmon, many of which come in a solid colour or are chrome and gold finishes. By adding blue you will imitate an ailwyfe or chartreuse and green are the colours of a shad. Depending what the fish's source of bait fish is that particular day will determine how successful you'll be that day.

ADD A PAIR OF EYES

Bucktail jigs is one of baits that showed improved performance. My method of presentation with bucktail jigs is called rip jigging, for both Bass and Walleye. Normally fishing dense weed areas is impossible. By simply adding a pair of prominent stick on eyes to a bait that otherwise appears very uninteresting to a fish. You can now imitate a feeding minnow and with a dab of fish scent and transform this jig into a magic bait.

ADD A RUBBER CORE SINKER

A lot of times I have found a specific floating bait is producing well, then it shuts off because the fish have moved to deeper water. To fish a little deeper I will add a 1/4 oz. rubbercore sinker to get to my desired depth. These sinkers reduce the risk of line damage compared to a conventional pinch-on weight. Connect about one foot in front of the lure up the line.

HOOK CHANGES

When considering a hook change you will want to try to keep as close to the weight that is equal to the treble hooks weight. This will not effect the action as much, if at all. Again, in reference to a bait where you are replacing a treble hook with a siwash hook: this will improve hook setting yet reduce injury due to multiple hooking on smaller fish.

Another recommended rig to consider a hook change on, is an ice fishing spreader. Lake Simcoe ice fishing hut operators include these when you use their services. It's been my personal preference to reduce the standard size 2 hooks to at least a size 6 or even an 8. In doing this you will be able to hook those smaller minnows without killing them. You can catch more fish on a livelier bait.

SPOONBILL ADJUSTMENTS

Before you put a flame to a spoonbill, be sure you understand it can only be done once. The reason you would do this is to change the running depth to either up or down. Your advantage is to get in the fish's FACE, to provoke a strike. Be sure to heat the plastic until it can be adjusted slightly.

SPLIT RINGS

The addition of a proper-sized split ring on a crankbait, on the front eyelet will give the bait an erratic action as well as a rattle by twitching your rod tip as you reel in. This is a real plus when trying to locate fish if your not using a sonar. It was suggested by a fishing friend to, pick certain lures, install a split ring and leave them on the lure.

LURE EYE-DENTIFICATION

For many years the best performing lures are those that manage to replicate a natural bait size, appearance and action. It would be futile to spend time using a lure that barely resembles a fish's natural forage. In my opinion, the colours, the finish, and, most importantly, the baits eyes must be properly positioned and be both bold and brightly coloured.

We have used split rings to produce a clicking noise and put on prisms to catch the fish's attention, now we find that there was something even more simple to get consistent action.

The next time you catch a fish on your favourite lure, whether its a jig head, a spinnerbait, crankbait or a spoon. Check to see if it has a huge pair of fish eyes, odds are it will.

Whenever you buy discounted lures, be certain they have a prominent pair of eyes. If the lure doesn't, don't waste your money.

A fish will instinctively take a minnow from underneath, just slightly behind it's eye. The reason for this is they use the minnow's eye as a target and this attack is in the bait fish's blind spot. If your imitation bait has small or no eyes, the striking fish will have no target. This produces a "short strike" or a miss.

If your bait is not producing, although you are feeling a number of hits, it's time to modify your baits by adding a pair of stick-on eyes or change to a better quality bait with big, bright and bold eyes.

When I plan to be "rip jigging" for gamefish, I always install a colour coordinated pair of stick-on prism (reflective) eyes on all my new bucktailed jigs. They react very well in comparison to the standard black dot eyes. To make the fish hang on to your baits longer, add a drop of Sparkle Scale liquid scent.

Most of the spinner baits I use are brightly coloured. To entice more strikes I add a pair of bright eyes or some scent.

Since I discovered this technique, I have been applying stick-ons to every kind of bait that looks unnatural. Before you head out on your next fishing trip sift through your lures and make up their eyes until they look gorgeous. You may be pleasantly surprised at your improved daily catch.

BAIT IMITATIONS

Gamefish thrive on minnows, worms, leeches, frogs, salamanders, crayfish, and both aquatic and flying insects as their main source of food. Obviously, from this you'll know the best baits are those that can imitate the shape, replicate the colours and duplicate the actions of natural baits as well as taste similar.

It's a fools game, although no one is really the fool. We are attempting to convince the fish into thinking that our artificials are natural bait. It is quite easy if you only use live bait. Unfortunately, nearly every time your bait is hit, it's either damaged or torn off.

With the price of live bait, it can and will become costly. To reduce our replenishing expenses, we can switch to reusable baits, artificials.

Such things as cut baits, made of pork hides, come shaped as frogs, lizards, crayfish and strips that look like eels and leeches. A popular choice of tournament professionals and most levels of serious angler's. Jigs and jelly baits are another substitute because they are durable and can be purchased in bulk. They are available in hundreds of colours, you can also buy them in minnow, grub, crayfish, leech, lizard and frogs.

You can virtually catch every species of freshwater fish from small to very large. One of fishing's most popular minnow imitations is Rapala's original. The inventor from Finland, hand crafted his lure out of balsa wood and painted them to closely resemble a bait fish. At Normark the distributor of this style of lure, has produced, pro-tested (by professional fisherman) and designed dozens of various depth and colours for every species of gamefish. Their popularity over the years is proof that imitation, replication and duplication are the key to success. The only thing that is required of you as an angler is the presentation when using this top producing bait.

In recent years there has been quite a number of lure companies that have matched and surpassed the quality of imitations. You can pay for this extreme quality and performance as much as ten dollars each.

Conventional tackle is still able to maintain preference and can be found in at least eight out ten tackle boxes. I'm referring to spinner baits, singleblade, tandem with willow leaves, Colorado and Indiana blades dressed with a hundreds of colour combinations in skirts and painted body weights.

In closing I would like to mention that times have changed in the price of tackle, now instead of saving your pennies, you'll have to save your "toonies" to fill your boxes.

A conventional tackle selection:
- RED AND WHITE BOBBERS • SPOONS AND SWIVELS
- HOOKS; ASSORTED • SPINNER BAITS
- SINKERS; DIFFERENT SHAPES AND SIZES • BEETLE SPINS
- INLINE SPINNERS • SPOOL OF LINE

NEVER ENOUGH TACKLE (making your own is easy)

Even though I enjoy fishing as much as the rest of you, there are times when I am sitting thinking of ways to increase my tackle supply. You can never have enough tackle.

While searching through the aisles of the Spring Fishing Show, I stumbled upon a man putting together a spinner similar to one that would have cost you five dollars in a tackle shop. Great, show me how you finish it off. This should not be difficult, or so I thought. All he did was pinch the main wire with a pair of needlenose pliers and twisted the running end around itself with his fingers keeping it tight, and just trimmed the excess off with side cutters. That was a lot simpler than I ever expected. What would that lure cost to make? By buying the components in groups of ten you can make them for approximately eighty cents each. My next question is will they work? If you are able to replicate any of the store bought brand name lures, there should be no reason why they shouldn't work.

What would impress me is being able to manufacture a variety of lures that will perform on as many gamefish as possible.

Last year I spent about two hundred dollars on specially selected components to make spinners for speckled and rainbow trout and I also designed some weight forward spinners for walleye. This order kept me selling spinners at both sportsmen shows and well into the fall. I wanted to tempt people by pricing them at ten dollars for a five pack. On the average, brand-named lures of equal quality would cost you at least four dollar each.

Although the colours and styles are limitless. I thought that by painting the body weights and colour co-ordinating them with the spinner blades I could double the selections. To even further enhance both the plain and coloured baits I started adding custom cut prisms to the top and underside of the blades. What else is there? Oh, how about coloured stick-on fish eyes for even better imitation and positive strikes?

In testing my personal designs I have produced a good number of speckled trout, rainbows, walleye and a few of the spinners were taking bass.

The other advantage was, all my lures were designed, assembled and tested by THIS professional fishing guide. By doing so, I could eliminate any lures that failed to produce, and concentrate on producing the performers. This season I plan to design and test a line of larger lures specifically for salmon, bass, pike and musky.

It only makes sense to me at this point to give them a name of their own to identify that they were made in Canada, Lynx Lure Designs.

It's sad but true, every fisher has the same old problem, people will only believe your fish stories if they are accompanied by a picture of fish with your lure still in it's mouth. Been there, done that!

HOOKED ON KNOW-HOW

I can honestly say that, every time I go fishing I learn something new about fish habitat, modifying techniques, presentations and selecting the best performing lures. I have come a long way since the first time I wet a line.

This important information for selecting terminal tackle (hooks, line & sinkers etc). Where, what, why and how to can be very helpful.

HABITAT As soon as you learn what is required for common environment for each species of fish, their holding patterns influenced by changing weather, their seasonal movements and spawning areas, you will have half the battle won.

FORAGE FOOD SOURCE Generally most species of fish are cannibalistic. Each body of water will have similar populations of frogs bait fish, crayfish, leeches and aquatic insects. If the bait gets scarce you may find them consuming their young for lack of food.

PRESENTATIONS The "KEY" to success is realizing where to cast and at what depth you'll want to get your bait to run at. To determine exactly what they are feeding on at the time of the day you're fishing to trigger a strike.

LURE SELECTION Once you have located your desired species, you should choose a lure that most replicates the indigenous species of bait fish; what they should be feeding on. When choosing your lure, it should also duplicate the action, Or imitate a wounded bait to provoke a strike. Try adding suitable scents. It's very important your bait can easily fit into a fish mouth. Generally, smaller is better.

HOOK SIZE On live bait presentations, your hook should be small enough that it can be concealed in the bait or choose bronze coloured or a black fine wire specialty hook.

ROD AND REEL CHOICES You can best decide if your conventional tackle will serve you or whether you will require specialty rods designed to perform on your specific species. As soon as you have a good understanding of the fish, tackle, where to look, and your best presentation to consider your level of confidence will rise and you might become obsessed with this fantastic sport as I have for over four decades. Been there, done that and even worn the hat.

NATURALLY LOCATING FISH

Are you paying attention when you are out on the water, particularly to the "fish birds'!

Herons, Loons, Seagulls (Harbour Turkeys), Kingfishers, Peregrine Falcons and Cormorants are all fish birds. It is very rare that they land, dive or swoop down to areas on lakes and rivers and come up empty handed. This generally is a positive indication there are either fish or bait fish in the vicinity.

Move closer and cast a lure past the school of bait fish that most resemble the minnows which are indigenous to the water, ie. Perch. Run your bait through the school with a stop and go retrieve to make your lure look like it's injured. By doing this your bait may become the easiest to eat in a fish's eyes.

Another thing to observe is bait fish taking insects from the surface. This indicates fish feeding which in turn may stimulate bigger fish to fee. Try this area with a top water or sub surface minnow bait or a popper cast past and slowly bring your bait to the school.

Angler's advantage is by wearing better quality polarized sun glasses. You may in a lot of cases be able to spot big fish or their silhouettes under water. You will be able to react using a plastic worm, grub or tube jig to stimulate a strike.

Another situation is when you are fishing shallow, thick or pencil weeds you can identify a fleeing fish by the ripple producing rail. You can quickly cast your bait in front of the trail and lift it up as the fish passes.

On a breezy day you can find feeding fish in the wave wash near the shoreline. This stirs up aquatic life such as insects and larvae. Try smaller weighted grubs or tubs jigs in bright colour, fish in at least ten feet of water, avoid coarse fish.

If you are faced with a cold front you will have to put away your crank baits and switch to slow moving finesse baits with a lighter weight to allow them to descend slowly. A 1/8 oz. jig head has worked very well into the past.

If you are working (fan casting towards the shore) a shoreline and there are no apparent takers, move out about ten (10) yards and fish the waters that are deeper, still towards the shore.

If you fish less than eights hours in a day you may not see as many of these signs. By now we all know that on the average most fish will feed aggressively twice a day. Although in a lot of cases the unsettled weather conditions will change their feeding patterns.

Rule of thumb: Wind from the east, fish bite the least; wind from the west, fish bite the best.

SUN STRESS

There are a number of reasons why some anglers prefer to fish on a cloudy day. The main one would probably be the damage that steady sunshine can cause. Here are some helpful tips that will protect us from some of the most prevalent harmful rays.

A full brimmed hat which has ventilating holes to allow the hot air to escape such as a "Tilley" hat can prove to be very effective. Although a traditional baseball cap is more popular because of its price tag and of course the fact that it can sometimes tell people that you are an interested fisherman because it says so on the embroidered crest. My fishing hats are the most essential pieces of equipment I carry when spending a day on the water.

Another preventive measure is to develop the habit of wearing "polarized" sunglasses with a high ultraviolet ray protection level, no less than 100% UV rating. Brand names to look for are, Bluewater Optics, Sarengetti and Hobie's.

With our UV exposure warnings announced daily it is wise to remember to always carry, as well as use a good sunscreen on exposed areas of skin. Neglecting to apply sunscreen can take the fun out of fishing in a very short time. Unfortunately no one has come up with a flavoured sun tan lotion as yet. So for now, we will have to protect our lips by using lip balms with some level of sunscreen added to it for minimal protection.

As a teenager, I learned the importance of being cautious after being badly burned and suffering from sunstroke I quickly started wearing a hat, sunglasses, lip balm and a 30 SPF sunscreen. My days of fishing

were always longer than several hours. If you are that enthusiastic that you must fish all day in the sun, be sure to take care out there!

SO, WHAT'S THE CATCH? (Adverse effects of changing weather)

Whenever I go fishing, as I get closer to the docks there are always a few people staring at me in disgust. The fact that I am sporting six to eight fishing rods and sometimes as many as four tackle boxes, probably has a lot to do with it.

I would like to try to explain the distinct adverse effects of changing weather throughout the seasons.

The fish's feeding habits are "triggered" by a number determining factors. Consistent weather, air and water temperature, cloud cover, wind direction and speed, barometric pressure, seasonal change and my favourite, lunar influence.

SPRING Spring brings up emerging aquatic life and insects which stimulates feeding bait fish. This in turn will make the bigger fish come out of hibernation to feed on both the minnows and the insects.

SUMMER The warming trends will eventually put a lake into a condition called "thermal balance". Once this occurs, the gamefish can be found where you should expect them, because they have finished spawning for this season. The term for this is referred to as "in position".

AUTUMN The fall brings in the onslaught of cooler weather. This is a sign to the fish that its time to feed more aggressively to bulk up for the long winter. The big fish will come into shallower water and begin preying on, bait fish, crayfish, leeches and in a lot of cases cannibalize their own.

Gradually the lakes go into a transition known as "flipping". This condition is where the water at the top of the lake has cooled to near the temperature of the water at the bottom of the lake. This effects fishing dramatically for an undetermined length of time.

WINTER The cold water will slow down the fish's feeding, from aggressive to a lethargic pace. By the time the lake freezes, their primary food source will be limited to bait fish only.

No matter what time of the year it is, you will be gathering a good selection of specific tackle to line the interior of your fishing boat.

Is there a need or is it overkill ?

To become proficient at every species of gamefish you would have to possess a good knowledge of each fish's preferred environment, food sources and their usual feeding times of the day. The best way to effectively compile this type of information is to spend a lot of time fishing the lakes that hold the highest population of the specific species of fish.

In order to produce fish consistently you will have to experiment with a number of live and artificial baits to determine what is the common food source they prefer. Once you establish that and as long as you are able to pinpoint the high percentage areas, you should remain consistent in producing more fish.

Persistence, perseverance and versatility can be your best confidence builders at any stage of the game

CHAPTER TWO
Game Fish Techniques

TREASURE MAPS FOR BASS

After several years of steady fishing, you would think that there was enough tackle and equipment in your arsenal to catch any size fish at any given moment. Check to see if you have a map library, just in case you have to pre-fish for a bass tournament. Maps are commonly over-looked and under rated.

My partners and I always use either a topographical or a hydrographic map to quickly eliminate unlikely areas to avoid wasting valuable time. As well, we can pencil in promising sections and concentrate on only the best producing areas during tournaments.

Bass hang around structure which creates constant shaded areas. They will also bury themselves in weedy areas. After feeding they may move into deeper pockets of water at the end of flats. These are called food shelves.

Their feeding habits generally dictate where you can locate them all day long. They are notorious for their ambush feeding methods. What they do is sit in the shade (trying to blend into the darkness), until a minnow, crayfish, frog, salamander (mud puppy), leech or an insect passes through their strike zone, then they quickly emerge from their hiding spot and literally inhale the bait.

Some areas to look for when trying to locate large populations of schooling bass are sunken islands, drop offs, rock faces with deep water, weed edges and points with a gradual decline in depth.

Maps can also assist us in locating marinas, launches, canals, resorts, causeways and the safest water routes. If you are forced to pull your maps out regularly, it's a good idea to have them laminated or store them in a zip-lock waterproof freezer bag.

Overall, maps can provide you with the important information you'll need to avoid boat and motor damage as well as the names of islands for future reference.

Something you may want to try is, use your sonar to mark and strategically place marker buoys to stay within a "hot" zone once you have located fish. If you are a cottager and you dare travel further away from your cottage areas; a map can simplify the trip. You may be pleasantly surprised at the amount of fish productive water you may have been missing over the years.

MAGIC BAIT FOR BIG BASS (Smallmouth)

Recently I had the pleasure of participating in a Chevy Truck/Mariner Pro Bass tournament with a very talented angler, Erny Janzen from St. Catherines. He and I managed to get in a day of pre-fishing in the Midland area and stumbled on a bait combination that put us near the top for the two day event. It's necessary to mention that without products from Ambush Tackle, we would not be able to fully develop this fantastic rigged presentation.

After spending most of the morning on Georgian Bay with my new found partner before the above mentioned pro tournament, Erny and I found ourselves literally turning our tackle storage systems (soft tackle boxes) inside out in an attempt to find a bait that would out perform the rest to aid us in coming in contention with the 75 teams participating.

After experimenting with top water, spinners and crankbaits; we couldn't manage to catch anything worthwhile. Although we had concluded that the largemouths were not where they should be at this time of season and that we would be forced to concentrate on smallmouths.

We were armed with a broad selection of scent impregnated and salt injected finesse baits and as many other plastic bodies to find the magic bait that would send the smallmouths into a feeding frenzy.

While we were fishing, I asked Erny if he had much luck in the past when using tube jigs. His comment was that the shorelines were covered with dead and moulted crayfish remains. From that information, it sounded like the way to go was to change to a crayfish imitation.

Bag 'o Bass...weighing in

We looked at each other, without exchanging any words. We both began changing our baits to a salted tube that we squirted with some Kick 'n Bass scent (inside the tube) then installed the jighead until it was all the way to the front of the tube. Then we began casting to points and into the shaded areas of these many sunken islands.

By hopping them back as if they were fleeing from predators, we managed to trigger numerous strikes. From the improved results, we decided that this unique rig was going to be the bait choice on tournament day. During a pre-fishing exercise, we were not attempting to hook any fish, just locate the better sized ones.

The specific areas we were fishing were flats and sunken islands, ranging from four to eight feet in mostly clear to somewhat murky waters. Under these ideal conditions, smallmouths will follow the bait until they are convinced it is food then aggressively attack it. Also, by hopping the bait back rather than letting it drop to the bottom, we were able to view the strike and throw a follow up cast if the fish did not take the bait.

Use four inch salted tube baits in a rootbeer or smoke colour and a #2 sized (owner) tube jighead. Also, use a little Kick 'n Bass spray scent inside the tube. It's real magic!!!

MAKING THE TRADE TO BRAIDED LINE (Superlines)

For the longest time I remained apprehensive about spooling up with braided line. There are a number of reasons, they are as follows:
1) very concerned that the line would damage my ceramic line guides.
2) also figured my reels would be destroyed beyond repair.
3) it was my belief that due to the extra strength of these lines, I would be breaking my rods regularly.

All of these concerns are common, in fact you could conceivably damage your equipment if you are not careful when adjusting your (reel) drag system. As far as I know, there has not been many complaints of damage while using braids. Although the manufacturers have not suggested the most effective, knot as of yet. Stren recommends the polymer knot finished by adding a drop of fast drying liquid glue called lock knot.

Recently I had an opportunity to switch from copolymer line (20# test) to 10/30 Power Pro (8 pound test diameter/breaking strength of 30# test). Experimenting during a bass tournament is not always wise, although I felt my bait casters were best suited for this kind of work out along with a couple of specialty rods we were planning to use for pitching and flipping presentations.

Shortly after blast-off (starting time) my partner and I arrived at a real promising area, with weed growth of about four feet in water six to eight feet deep. This is a prime area for amazing largemouth bass. We both believed that it should be holding lots of above-average sized bass. All we had to do is figure out which bait presentation was going to stimulate the most strikes.

We started with one of us using a buzz bait and the other used a spinner bait. After about five minutes, we switched to a Bass-Assassin (a finesse bait, soft plastic) and I used a Super Zara-Spook.

So far nothing was working, then we switched again to a jig & pig and a Texas rigged lizard saturated with some Kick 'n Bass scent. Finally the fish began to turn on. Between the worm rig and the lizard we put over five fish in the boat. Unfortunately I kept breaking off as

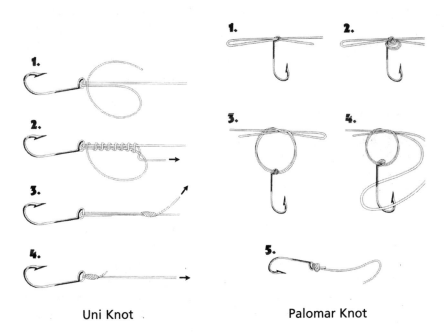

Uni Knot   Palomar Knot

my knots were failing on the hook sets. This was costing us a number of good sized bass. Experimenting during a Pro-level tournament is not a thing I would normally practice.

My partner showed me a fail-safe knot that had worked for him in the past. It put an end to my disappointment and put me right back on track. As far as any of my equipment suffering any damage, the braid seemed to be no more damaged than polymer line, except that the braided line has near zero stretch in it; a property that increases the chances of hair trigger hook set. Being able to escape from the fear of the unknown has opened my eyes to the obvious advantages of using braided line. Occasionally new products last no longer than one turn on the shelf and sometimes as long as two years. After testing this and observing its many superior properties such as, super strength, less than 5% stretch, virtually no memory and it won't become damaged over time by the ultraviolet sun rays. It does not have to be changed as often as conventional line and you can spool up from one reel to another to start fresh. Next season I plan to use braided line on all the bait casters to develop my self-confidence with hopes that the new knot won't give up on me at all.

BOUNCING FOR THE BIG ONES

One thing that gets my adrenaline flowing is catching a fish that is bigger than your best, especially if its pulled off using a new method of presentation.

Most of the lakes I frequent when guiding are termed as "land locked "or pocket lakes. This means they don't have a stream or river flowing in or out of them. Typically lakes of this nature are capable of producing a good number of average sized fish ranging from two to five pounds. They will also hold better fish, although there will be less of a population. To catch these brutes, you can choose your best options. Deep running crank baits, the use of heavier line weights or downrigging.

Last year while fishing a deeper lake that has all kinds of structured areas. I found myself rummaging through my tackle box trying to find some sinkers. I stumbled upon a package of three-way swivels and a 3/4 oz. bottom bouncing rig. An idea came to me. "If I rig up the weight with a minnow imitation it will put the offering directly in the fish's face." This would involve snipping off about a two foot leader line to run from the three-way swivel. Tie the end of the main line to one side of the swivel, the other tie on the leader line and the lower ring can be fastened to the bouncing weight. My lure choice was a AC shiner (floating) three inch minnow in a silver body with a black back. A floating lure should run approximately one foot off the bottom. Perfect position for triggering a strike.

After tying everything together you should drop it into the water to make sure it runs straight. Then let out about fifty feet of line behind the boat, engage the free spool and get ready for the upcoming strike. Pay close attention to your fish locator, try to position your boat to take you through schools of fish. What I do when trolling, rather than troll in a straight line I continuously cut in towards the shore and before it gets too shallow cut back out. This technique automatically changes your lure speeds. The angler on the inside of turn realizes a slower speed and the angler on the outside of the turn will feel an increase in speed. Both can and will trigger a more aggressive strike.

On the day I tried this method I got a vicious strike within the first five minutes. It was about a seven pound walleye. With the extra weight of the bottom bouncing rig I thought I was into the biggest fish in the lake. On a positive note, it added to the level of excitement.

This technique has worked very well on other gamefish since then. Be sure to bring along a larger landing net to avoid disappointment. Those stories about the one that got away are only believable if you can bring yourself to tears when telling your tale.

Musky Brother!

EXPLOSIVE TOP WATER LURES

There are a number of reasons why I am drawn to fish again and again. It seems that the Ontario lakes in the morning can bring a sigh of relief to every suburban dweller. The fresh air can fill your lungs to give you a new hidden energy and the sounds of nature seem to harmonize like no other area of beauty.

With all this and then to be able to see the water boil up around your lure, presented primarily for Bass and regularly it could be taken by a Northern Pike or a Musky is even more exhilarating.

George Gouvianakis, Dan Sturges' fishing buddy

There are at least a half dozen different top water baits that create high levels of excitement for me nearly every time I venture out.

BUZZ BAIT: This noisy rig has an amazing affect on small and Largemouth Bass. The suggested trick for making this bait work is speed changes and short jerking motions. In the case of Bass striking, they will hit because it provokes them, a reaction bait.

SPINNER BAIT: These baits can come in a variety of different configurations mainly by adding or changing the spinner blade shapes. They are often cased and immediately retrieved, burned back to your rod tip, slow rolled (fast enough to keep it just off the bottom) or crank and paused to get a hit.

ZARA SPOOK: A torpedo shaped bait with a rattle chamber big bold and bright eyes. The technique for presenting this bait is to pause long enough after casting it, until all the ripples on the water are gone. Then start by reeling and twitching your rod to make it dodge from side to side. This is called"Walking the Dog". Pause for at least two seconds once struck, then lean into the hook set with your medium heavy rod tip.

SPITTIN" IMAGE: Relatively new on the market, although unique in its presentation. A smart fish's first choice.

SKIDDER POP: Rapala's first top water artificial with a broader colour spectrum. This is retrieved in a similar manor, also implies a recovering injured minnow.

HUSKY JERK: Be sure it is not a suspending type bait. Cast and retrieve with a longer stroke, it appears as if it has spotted it's predator making a run for it.

Although these are the top producing lures of choice, do not focus on only these models. There are many more out there. To effectively introduce these types of baits, you will have to use a medium to heavy one piece, bait casting rod and reel combination and at least #17 test mono or copolymer fishing line.

BOAT SIDE MANNERS (Stuck on Stupid)

I am sure we've all had at least one depressing story to tell about,"the fish that got away!" In a majority of cases the problem stemmed from human error. As in every sport, we all get to learn from our mistakes.

To improve as an angler or as an assistant to an angler, there are a couple of things to remember.

A common reaction created by the high level of excitement is panic. Whenever this occurs we can find ourselves trying to win the race of getting our fish in first or horsing the fish to the point of breaking our line. The biggest mistake is assuming that your fishing line will not break if you try to lift the fish into the boat without a net.

Failing to tie an effective fishing knot, such as an improved clinch knot or a polymer knot and neglecting to moisten them before you snug them down. Both of these knots have been tested for wet knot strength and are classed as the best when either monofilament or copolymer is used.

It's really bothersome to see anyone pinch on their sinkers using pliers rather than their teeth. This action generally creates damage to the breaking strength of their line. A nick can reduce the breaking strength by well over fifty percent.

Someone I know, still manages to lose eight out of ten of his fish because he fails to understand the importance of the shock absorption property of his fishing rod when angling a fish to the boat side.

Another common mistake is, that after managing a couple of fish into the boat it is good practice to cut off a foot or two of line and retie. This will reduce the inevitability of line failure due to abrasion.

When your fish is big enough to bring out a net, be sure to ease the fish's "head" into the net rather than chase it's tail. Delegate your partner as your net person. Inform them that you will signal them when you want your fish scooped up.

Proper specific handling of each species of fish is important for improved mortality rates. Bass, by the bottom lip, trout and salmon (when fishing a stream) should be beached carefully and tail them from a boat. Walleye, push down their dorsal fin and grip them snugly across their back. When handling the toothy characters (musky and pike), place one hand across their back behind their gill plates and the other should be wrapped around the fish right in front of the tail while someone else removes the hooks.

All game fish should be played quickly, admired, then gently released so other anglers can do the same another day. Recycle, Re-hook, and return!

THE IMPORTANCE OF BOAT CONTROL

If you want to use your time effectively when fishing you'll want to concentrate on productive areas only. This does not mean you head for the same location and drop anchor. To do so you are going to have to "work the lake", to determine if the fish are where they should be or if they are on the bite or shut down.

As you enter a potential holding area, come in slow and quietly. Refrain from dropping the anchor and stop your motor. Start dropping marker buoys instead. After detecting a strike and positioning a marker, as you DRIFT out of the strike zone. Start up your motor and make a wide circle to just in front of your marker. Do this until the fish stop biting, then move to another holding area. Keep repeating this until you run out of markers. Leave the markers in the best areas and plan on returning a little later (about and hour). If you go out of sight of the markers, then you should collect them to avoid having them disappear on you. All the time you are searching for bigger fish be versatile by changing your presentations to what might be more suited to the species of choice.

You start off the day by finding a breeze that blowing in the right direction as well at a perfect speed early in the day. I call this fishing with Mother Nature, in a sense letting her be in control of your boat. As this progresses the wind direction will probably change so you may be forced to move out of the area or switch back to controlling your boat with your motor.

Other conditions you may be faced with are no breeze at all. When I am in this situation I start my motor and troll in reverse to keep moving slow but continuing to cover lots of water.

If you are using #6 or #8 test line and a 1/4 oz. walking sinker with a BB sized split shot pinched on, 18 inches up from a #10 hook, your presentation will be right in the strike zone of bigger fish because they require deeper colder water which is higher in oxygen.

A popular fishing aid device is an electric positioning motor. It is quiet, simple to operate, and inexpensive. In comparison with a gas engine it works just as well but without the noise. If you don't solely rely on them, they can last longer than a day. Working the structure areas such as drop offs, weed lines, tree falls and shaded areas under overhanging trees, boat houses and docks. You can also use a depth finder to locate underwater structure such as flats, humps, sunken islands, weeds and bait fish.

All the time you are trying to locate productive areas of any lake you will understand how foolish it is to expect the fish to come to you.

If you are having to deal with swifter winds you can point the bow into the breeze and maintain a speed of just over a standstill. This may not be your idea of fun so you can move to the leeward side of an island to shield yourself from the winds. Consistently a depth of 18 to 24 ft will produce almost every kind of gamefish.

Being a little more adventurous, I have challenged a fishing buddy to pursue some trophies from a canoe. The breeze can work for you while searching some key ambush areas such as, lily pads, weed mats, and around fallen waterlogged trees or through a boulder area. Or you can completely change your tactics to go after musky or pike. Select bigger lures to catch bigger fish, you could try a new Husky Jerk from Rapala or a Smithwick Rattlin' Rogue and maybe a 6" Slug-go a popular finesse bait.

There have been a few times I can remember that a huge fish took my bait and absolutely exploded while fishing from a canoe. Being literally attacked, which scared me into realizing, either I capsize risking major tackle loss or bailing out of the canoe to subdue my quarry standing waist deep in the water.

Sometimes while drifting past other anglers I will ask, "how is the fishing today"? Sadly enough after releasing several big fish minutes before hand, after working the lake. I respond by suggesting that they pull up their anchor and let the breeze take them to the fish. Also to keep in around 15 to 20 ft of water for best results. You would soon give up this wonderful sport if all you ever caught was one mediocre fish every time you went fishing. Fishing is supposed to be fun, so, — make it so Jean Luc.

WALK-ON-WATER? (Installing a walking deck on your boat)

One of my fishing buddies and I were having a conversation while returning from a great day of fishing. We were discussing the possibility of installing a walking deck in his new Lund aluminum boat. We felt that we could become more comfortable, less cluttered and it would help us become more versatile when casting and landing fish because we fish together all the time, we agreed to share the cost of the upgrades.

When first assessing the job you may think it is going to be difficult. My brother and I customized his boat a few years ago so we at least have an idea what we'll need for materials. The hardest part was drawing up the plans so there wouldn't be any holes drilled into the hull of the boat. We wanted it to be durable and light weight. Before we knew it, we were in a lumber store selecting some nice pieces of marine plywood, some cedar 2x4's, contact cement and some brass hinges. The indoor outdoor carpeting we chose matched the interior walls of the boat. We decided to bridge the floor area to create a level walking surface throughout. By covering the existing seat boxes with plywood and carpeting them. We could stay colour coordinated. This would give us the needed strength to install our boat seats.

Before the Blast Off

In the front of the boat between the bow and the front seat, we decided to recess into the floor an old cooler that I made into a livewell. Lucky for us, it also accommodated our deep-cycle batteries too. This could supply power to the trolling motor and sonar. At the stern of the boat, behind the rear seat, became an ideal storage area for the fuel tank and the rope and anchor. Then by installing a swivel seat we would have the option of standing or sitting while fishing. Opposite that, we mounted our sonar where it could always be in view of the driver. Because we use floatation cushions along with our P.F.D.'s, they would always be handy under our backsides. To hold our rods in place while we were moving, we bought two short bungee straps and bundled them to the gunwale so the could not fall overboard. This design would eliminate a majority of noise that was caused by beverage cans, pliers, fishing rods and placement of equipment. It was an advantage to us that with a deep "V" hull the extra weight of the walking deck was less than a third passenger. It didn't effect the handling nor the stability.

Being careful when choosing the colour of the carpet actually made the job look like it was purchased as a package. Not only does this simple modification add to the overall appearance, it also increases the resale value by nearly a thousand dollars. I would have liked to have included the building plans, but they were drawn up to fit a Lund boat. A few careful measurements, some calculations and I'm sure you will be well on your way to customizing your own boat.

TRY RIP JIGGING

After experimenting all last season with this unique presentation, I convinced myself that its excellent for catching above average bass as well as walleye. As usual I felt it was necessary to modify the baits to increase productivity.

Start with a handful of 1/4 oz. bucktailed (banana type) jig heads in white, black, yellow or gold, using a spinning outfit with a medium action tip, spooled with premium clear coloured fishing line 10# test ie. Super Silver Thread or Excalibur. If you prefer, use a baitcasting combo with 14# test.

To prepare your baits remove the paint from the eye hole, then buy a package of stick on prism eyes and place them over the existing painted eyes. Next, apply a liberal amount of bait fish scent to the tail of your jig. By tying direct, your bait will appear more natural and produce consistently.

Locate an area that has thick sparse weed growth or an isolated cove that is primarily weeds. Begin fan casting into open pocket areas or into the shaded areas of the weeds. Let your bait touch bottom each time you complete a cast, holding your rod tip close to the surface of the water, pull the bait quickly through the weeds in short strokes retrieving the slack line each time. When you feel an interruption, pause a few seconds, then set the hook in an upward motion.

It's been my personal opinion for a very long time, your best advantage as an angler is to wear a good pair of polarized sunglasses to avoid missing many fish that you would otherwise not see using the naked eye. You will find a lot more ambushing fish if you concentrate on fishing weeded areas with a depth of at least six to eighteen feet. Also be careful to observe that the weeds are healthy. This will dictate a high content of oxygen and assure an abundance of bait fish which in turn promotes a better population of bigger fish.

When casting, it is important to cast low to allow quiet entry to avoid spooking the fish. If you get snagged in any weeds, position your boat directly over the snag and pull straight up until you're free. This way, you just have to get off the weed you are hooked on, rather than having to take on the whole field. It is common that both species tend to "bulldog" as soon as they realize they are hooked. For this reason, it is wise to actually horse the fish out of the hole by holding your rod at about one o'clock the entire time you are playing it. It is very important to set your drag a little tighter than normal. I hope you have as much fun with this method as I have!

FANTASTIC PLASTIC

No matter how slow the fishing, if you choose most any plastic body/jig (grub) combination you should come up with an above average fish. Some anglers feel it is necessary to attach snaps swivels or a leader when tying on jigs. When actually doing this only hinders the performance of this type of bait, the truth of it is that by "tying direct" you are creating your most natural presentation. The best way to present a jig and body bait (grub) is by color coordination as well as jig head weight, being careful in selecting a good quality jig head that has a painted on realistic eye and a razor sharp hook which can make all the difference, ie. yellow body (3in.)with a yellow 1/4 oz.jig head or a white body (2in.) with a 1/8 oz. pink jig head or a black body (3in.)

All day long. Tube Jig again!

with a black 3/8 oz. jig head. Depending on how aggressive the fish are that day, a lighter jig head descends slower.

There are several presentations using grubs that have been working well for me over the years. By simply casting near and around different types of structure such as tree-falls, in drop offs at the end of shallow flats (at least eight feet or as much as thirty feet) just past the depth transition, in shaded areas under low lying docks, behind boulders or at either end of sunken islands where depths that are gradual. These areas are referred to as "high percentage" locations.

To avoid scaring (spooking) the fish, remember to cast a couple of feet past your intended areas, let your bait sink for approximately one second per foot, then bring your bait through the fish strike zone (just above it's head yet within view). On your second cast, do the same, but allow the bait to reach the bottom, here you would jig the grub back to your boat although, if you detect a hit, drop your rod tip quickly, reel in the slack line and set your hook. By using this method you will increase your percentages of positive hook sets by giving the fish a few seconds to actually close it's mouth on the bait.

A great method that teases and provokes fish to strike is, cast out as you would normally, allow the bait to hit bottom, then gently hop the bait towards you about five times, then quickly retrieve it with frequent short pauses to make it appear to be saying," Na,Na,Na,Na,Na, you can't catch me!" Pay close attention to your line as any interruption will probably be a fish. Don't be surprised if you get a fierce strike, one where you have to adjust your grip when an aggravate fish "Slams" your bait.

If you are a confident angler I would suggest a premium six pound test fishing line to reach optimum performance levels when using jigs. Still sure of your angling skills then consider using eight to ten pound test line. One of the best rod and reel choices is a graphite rod, six and a half foot, medium action, (fast tip) one piece rod, married with a balanced spinning reel (zero anti-reverse)of equal quality you will be able to finesse very effectively using a fast tip rod because it creates a more methodical jigging action while retrieving plastic baits. If you choose to rig the grub tail up you will get more strikes during the retrieve, although if you prefer to rig it with the tail down, you will experience more of your strikes during the descent. Either way will get you constant strikes. Adding a couple of drops of scent to each bait has always helped improve the numbers of fish per day!

VERTICAL JIGGING!

It seems everyone has a selection of matching coloured twister tails and jig heads in their tackle boxes. Although there is a number of different ways to present these artificial baits under ideal and inclement conditions. The most common is the vertical jigging method.

Once you consider an area that looks like it should be holding good fish, you can manoeuvre your boat to about three metres away from the hole and anchor there. Start by fan casting throughout the area and by pulling up your anchor you can to drift to the next hole and repeat the application. A piece of important equipment you might take with you most of time is a sonar. With it on board, you will be able to locate structured areas such as food shelves, sunken islands, drop offs and points. This will maximize your percentages of producing lots of big fish for the better part of the day.

To effectively present your baits, select a 1/4 oz. to 3/8 oz. jig head and dress your hook with either a Berkley Power Grub in black or white. Both the Jighead and the grub should be similar in colour to give the most natural presentation. Try to keep the colours the same or very close to make it look more natural. One of my favourites is a camouflage coloured Berkley Power Tube with the jig installed inside the tube or outside by using a yellow jig head. They work extremely well because they replicate a fleeing crayfish.

Another popular choice is using a bucktailed jig in a 3/8 to a 1/2 ounce with a drop of gamefish Kick 'n Bass original garlic fish attractant rubbed into the tail. The better producing colour choices have been, white, yellow and black. Followed up with a jig and minnow shad in black and silver three inches long, also with a drop of fish scent.

Last season I was experimenting with a 1/2 oz. Luhr-Jensen crippled herring in a natural colour. But I first dipped it in fish scent, I was pleasantly surprised by a four and half pound walleye while I was fishing for Largemouth bass.

On a day the fish have been thrown off the bite, due to a cold front moving into the area, you might want to devote most of your day to using the vertical jigging presentation. A majority of times it will be the only thing that can provoke a strike. My theory is, that one big fish is more exciting than ten little ones.

I caution you to try not to get hung up in one area too long. If a fish is going to strike, it should hit on the initial cast or its not going to hit at all. However if you manage a good fish or two, don't be afraid to drop a coloured marker to pinpoint the "honey hole" for later.

Use your sonar upon the return, as the fish tend to move with the bait fish, in and out. Don't forget to change your baits constantly if they are not performing. Personally, I will give a bait about five casts in a prime location, then switch. On the other hand if the bait does work. I will suggest everybody in the boat switches. If the fish move into deeper water, drop anchor and tie off when you have drifted over top of them. On an off day, be sure to give this method a try.

JIG AND TRAILER RIG

For many years Bass anglers have been tempting big hogs out of cover by using skirted jigs dressed with pork frogs, pork craws. Although they produce extremely well when using dark colours (black or blues) I have

FISHING FACT   Winds from the east, fish bite the least.
Winds from the west, fish bite the BEST!!

discovered a new technique using bright same coloured skirt jig to tempt finicky Musky and Pike.

You may have heard the term "big bait for big fish" often times. Well that is a good expression but what is big? Here is how you do it!

Pick out a brightly coloured rattling weedless jig and colour match it to a pork leech, ie. Yellow Skirted jig and a yellow pork eel (6" long). Cast it into potential area that my be holding Pike or Musky, let it decent to the bottom, and then lift your rod and begin rapidly retrieving your bait. When you encounter a strike, stop, drop and sweep set your hook. Do not give the fish any slack during your entire fight. If your fish decides to bullet out of the water and you are able to see if it is well hooked, then play the fish back to your boat by burying your rod in the water up to right in front of your reel. This reduces the fish's chances of breaking water by changing your playing angle. If you are able to entice a fish to follow up, begin a figure of Eight motion as quick as you can. I have had fish follow-up and performed the figure of eight. To increase your chances if he just sits and watches, slow it down and then push the free spool to allow your bait to head to the bottom. If the fish rejects your final offer, quickly change your rod to a Crankbait, cast well past the fish in the direction he exits and return your bait by imitating a wounded (Minnow) bait fish followed by an attempt to flee. After chasing the previous offer a wounded bait will be the Sushi of the day.

When fishing for predator type fish, you can fish using a leader (black) although while experimenting with the jig and pork you will trigger more strikes by using stronger fishing line and a bait casting reel with a medium heavy action rod, because you will be using a little larger than normal bait more of your hook sets will be around the lip area rather than down its throat.

Only remove the fish from the water if you plan to keep them. Otherwise try to remove the hook(s) along side your boat.

FISHING (Using Common Scents)

Have you have ever tried using fish attractants and found that they did not work all that well for you? Maybe you applied the wrong scent to your artificial.

When I head out for a day of fishing, you will find four different kinds of scents in my tackle bag. bait fish, crawfish, trout and original scent. The bait fish scent is used for applying to minnow imitations such as crankbaits, soft finesse baits or top waters. The crawfish scent should only be applied to crawfish imitating baits provided they haven't already been scented at the manufacturer. Trout scent does well on roe bags and on spoons or spinners. The original scent is designed to work on larger gamefish such as Northern Pike and Muskies.

The important thing to note is to apply the scent on the bait where it will be most effective. Here are some guide lines you may want to follow:

BAIT FISH SCENT It is wise to avoid applying the scent directly to the bait fish coloured areas of any of your crankbaits, because they are generally oil base. Not only will it fade the colour, it can alter the action and it can become less visible to the fish. Try applying your scent on the treble hooks or to the underside of the spoonbill. On spinner baits you can put a couple of drops on the hoola skirt. If you plan to use plastic minnow imitations, try soaking six or eight of them in a zip-loc sandwich bag over night. Use just enough to saturate the baits, half a teaspoon.

CRAWFISH SCENT You can apply this scent to crawfish coloured lures in a crankbait model as described above or an unscented plastic crawfish,all over it and my favorite, tube jigs either inside the tube before you insert the jighead or give it a little squirt on the top of the tube before you cast it.

ORIGINAL SCENt This is applied to larger baits used for tempting Northern Pike and Muskies. When using larger baits you may want to concentrate on the back treble hook and slop it on liberally.

TROUT SCENT If you use artificial spawn (Trout or Salmon eggs) you can apply some scent to the spawn sack material nearest to the not. For in-line spinners or spoons, saturate the treble hooks only. If you are float fishing using flies, adding a drop of scent to the first split shot sinker. This may get a fish to react to your fly presentation. In some cases you could be faced with a day where the fish are feeding aggressively. On these days you may get away with not using scents at all. Experiment with it!

MY FAVORITE LURES

There isn't one lure that out performs on every species, although there are always at least a couple that will work best for you on each species of game fish. Here are the ones that work well for me during tournaments (Bass) and while guiding clients the other game fish.

KING SALMON: Casting from shore or flat lining, a #7, jointed Rapala in chartreuse in a river mouth area is a good performer as well as a Little Cleo, size 1/4 oz. in either green or blue and silver. On a day where the water is murky, try a Bomber Thinfin Shad.

DOWNRIGGING: Northern King Mags in silver with blue or green prism tape. If you are forced to go deep, use a Lyman cut plug in a glow-in-the-dark pink or pearl. I have found that a lure presentation will get more aggressive strike action if apply a popular fish scent before wetting your line.This gives you all the features for fooling the "BIG" fish.

RAINBOW TROUT-STREAM FISHING CHOICES: Krocodiles in a 3/8 oz.with a pink, pearl or blue prism on a silver spoon. Also a brass or silver in-line spinner size one or two blade, look for a Mepps, Panther Martin's, Double Loon or Blue Fox. On a sunny day in clear water use any bright colored"dressed" Panther Martin with silver or gold blades in a size 2 to 9. If these don"t work as well as you like them to, switch to a 1/4 oz.jig and grub with a pink jig head dressed with a white Berkley's Power grub or a red jig and a black grub.

MUSKY: Although I prefer to cast to high percentage areas rather than troll. My preferred lure choices are first and foremost I will go with brightly colored (yellow or chartreuse) Buck-tail spinners in gold or silver, size 5, 6 or 7 and add a drop or two of fish attractant. Blue Fox and Lynx spinners are the good ones. Also Rapala's Husky Jerks (suspending) in gold or silver with black backs HJ14 size. An alternative bait is a jointed Swim Wiz with a white belly or some of Leo Lures can provide to be the wake up call for really big muskies.

NORTHERN PIKE: Casting baits such as Smithwick's Rattlin'Rouges or Rapala's Husky Jerk baits in a Fire Tiger or perch colour 5 inch size. A good quality spinner bait with large willow leaf blades and a scented trailer, can be your best choice fishing above weed tops.

TROLLING: Large spoons such as a Mepps Cyclops or a Five of Diamonds will get you into something almost immediately. Less aggressive fish will require a large deep diving bait such as a Deep Suspending Rattlin'Rouge in a bait fish colour.

WALLEYE: Some deadly baits are Cotton Cordell, Wally Diver in Chrome/black in a size CD5, this bait is designed to run at about twelve to fifteen feet. It would be wise to fish it in eighteen to twenty-two feet of water to keep your lure in their strike zone. Another deep diving bait is a Rapala's, Rattlin'Fat Rap in a perch colour. Finally Excalibur's, Fat Free Shad again with the rattle in their crawdad colour.

SMALLMOUTH AND LARGEMOUTH BASS: I prefer to fish "Top Water" lures such as a Zara Spook, a Pop-R and most recently Excalibur's, Spit'n'Image in a 3 1/4 in. Shad colour(DFTS)signature series.

SPECKLED TROUT: In a stream, a silver or gold Mepps in-line spinner, size "00" to size one. In a lake I use Panther Martins in a 1/8 oz. in a fluorescent orange with a silver blade (dressed). You will find this bait to perform more consistently if you let it sink almost to the bottom before you begin retrieving.

Although these baits can be found at your favorite tackle shops, it will still be up to you to experiment with different speeds and methods of retrieving to get them to perform for you. My recommendations for these lures are based on fishing under normal weather conditions.

If you should tell a friend that you were fishing with a Husky Jerk, explain to them that I might be husky but, I'm no JERK!

PITCHIN', FLIPPIN' AND DUNKIN'

1998 has brought with it a golden opportunity my way. My partner (alleged) for the Chevy Track Mariner Marine Pro Bass Tour bailed out on me after verbally agreeing to partner up the entire season. Luckily though, my good friend George Gouvianakis agreed to participate with me after the first tour of the season. This still left me without a partner. An option when a few of us are left to deal with this crisis is, we can be put on a list of available anglers and be drawn first come, first served.

I received the phone call on the Thursday before the tourney with only one day of pre-fishing allowed. The tournament director informed me that a top twenty Pro Anglers had requested that I fish both days as well as pre-fish the Friday with him.

My partner was Wes Lavergne of "Lets Talk Fishing" an excellent Pro Bass Angler for a number of years. We teamed up near Bobcageon at the locks and immediately set out to reduce unproductive waters and key in on locations that were holding primarily big fish. The idea is to catch five sizable fish ranging from two to three and a half pounds (a limit) then cull (remove the smallest fish and replace it with a better fish) until all five fish weigh a least four pounds.

We began with our bait casters, each rigged with a different bait. Until we determined which presentation was the most effective. Our options were a buzz-bait, Bass Assassin (finesse type bait), a spinner bait and Texas rigged worm and a jig and pig.

Generally, a spinner bait will consistently produce on any given day, however, that day was not one of those. The Bass Assassin nor the Slug-gos also could not get a reaction, this left us trying a buzz-bait. It

TOP WATER

SUB-SURFACE

DEEP DIVERS

SUSPENDING BAITS

did not work either. Neatly we began pitching into weed pockets with each of us using a different rig, Wes had a salted paddle tailed worm, Texas rigged and I used a jig and pig. Just as if someone had rung the dinner bell the fish turned on. It was obvious that a Texas rigged worm was the reactionary bait. I immediately changed to a Texas rigged lizard in blue fleck, saturated with some Kick'n Bass (garlic) fish attractant. After destroying six separate baits a strange feeling came over me, I was out of plastic lizards. Luckily there was a back up in a similar colour, a Berkley six inch curly tailed Power Worm. Important note. Use a marker buoy to keep you on the area.

Using the natural speed of the breeze we could dunk the holes more than pitch them. The Bass are commonly in tight to the bottom of these weeds, ready to attack as soon as some sort of forage passes through their strike zone. These congested weed areas are overlooked constantly although by using weedless rigged baits, you can have some explosive times beyond belief. The feeding frenzy could last an hour or it could go on for considerably longer. Fifteen minutes of no action has been a sign that it's over.

After culling (switch) several smaller fish, it was time to go get some really big fish to bring up our finishing weight. This was when we had to hook into (securely) some four pound plus fish. To effectively achieve our goal some long accurate pitches to shoreline slop, shaded low lying docks, boathouses and beneath moored boats should be our high percentage areas. My partner managed two good ones while I had not one take.

Although we should have had nearly fifteen pounds, the few missed fish kept our daily weight to just under eleven pounds. We could have finished around tenth spot had we successfully hooked everyone of the strikes from above average fish.

MAKE EVERY CAST COUNT!

The main contributing factor for any advancing angler is the ability to develop his or her accuracy at hitting crucial targets consistently when casting a variation of baits.

It has taken me many years to be able to pinpoint high percentage areas using only the naked eye, particularly when fishing unfamiliar bodies of water. Although not all of us are fully equipped with the new technologies, such as depth finders, temperature gauges, G.P.S. and electric positioning motors.

What you can look for is, underwater structure, actively feeding fish breaking water to take insects, or frogs. Birds such loons, kingfishers, herons, osprey and seagulls are great natural signs that schools of bait fish are in the area. These signs are good indications that there will be bigger fish monitoring these areas, ready to begin or continue feeding aggressively.

By accurately delivering similar artificial bait types, just past the active spots and retrieving the bait through the key areas may prove as a very effective approach. Some other obvious signs to look for are, shallow flats that drop off into deeper dark holes that tend to hold hungry ambushing fish waiting to strike at the first appearance of its preferred bait. Shaded areas in the shallows can create ideal ambush points for big "holding" fish. Under tree falls, behind boulders, and the shaded sides of tree covered islands are a consistent holding location for actively feeding fish. Try under docks which are closer to the surface and may include moored boats, as long as they provide shaded areas. Shaded areas can be casted into directly, using a sinking bait such as a Texas rigged worm or a Jig 'n Pig. Deeper areas will require a descending bait presentation like a tube jig in a natural colour and with a grub in either white or yellow.

CASTING STYLES

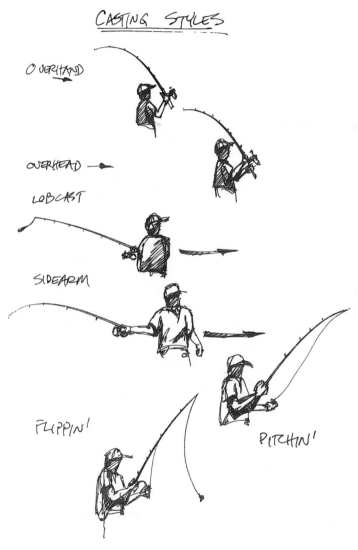

OVERHAND

OVERHEAD

LOBCAST

SIDEARM

FLIPPIN'

PITCHIN'

Once you decide on an area, cast past it, then bring your bait through the strike zone slowly to avoid spooking any fish. This also creates a more natural presentation. A trick I practice is, as you bring it through, change the movement of the bait to provoke a more aggressive and explosive strike. When it comes to heavy matted or weeded areas, your casting ability can be the determining factor on whether you hook up with a fish or go home disappointed.

FISHING THE WEEDS

Many anglers still refuse to consider fishing any type of weed cover, in fear of spending more time getting frustrated with snags and low productivity levels.

Conventional spinning tackle is not suited for fishing heavy cover. A bait casting rod and reel combination (one piece, medium to heavy action tip) spooled with at least 17# test premium fishing line is more specialized.

For anglers who have never tried this type of fishing, the transition has been known to lower self-confidence. With the many features available on the reels, take some time and accept advice from the sales staff. Be sure to get a complete demonstration which should include adjustments to the drag systems. Generally, first time buyers think the reel handle should be on the same side as their spinning outfit. This isn't true because you'll be using that hand to stabilize your equipment when playing any fish.

After practicing several times in the back yard, you may be ready to attempt to try the weeded areas. You will have to arm yourself with a variety of top water and weedless baits, such as Moss-Bosses, Zara Spooks, Hoola Popper, Chug Bugs, Torpedo, a Johnson Silver Spoon and some Slug-Gos. You'll do well by starting off with a tandem bladed spinnerbait, then progress to weedless jig and pig or use a cut-bait frog or crayfish.

In the fact that you will be presenting your baits fairly close to your boat as well as contending with the weeds regularly, you will be switching from a sweeping hook set to an upward hook set. To get these brutes out of the weeds, you have to horse them as quickly as possible or they will "bulldog" themselves into and around the base of the weeds in an effort to break you off.

Now we can switch to a Johnson Silver Spoon, dressed with a Pork Frog (called a trailer). This is a simple presentation, cast into the weeds and bring it back slowly, pause, reel a few times, then jiggle the bait, them bring it all the way back. Try to cover as much area as you can before moving on. When you see a boil (a fish surfacing to take the bait), wait until you can feel the fish pulling, then set the hook.

Probably the most popular bass bait used extensively throughout North America is the spinner bait. Since its inception it has helped more professional bass anglers win tournaments than any other artificial. Spinner baits were designed to run weedless, although they will prove you wrong every so often. You can improve their performance by adding such things as, a trailer hook, a colour matched trailer and a few drops of bait scent. You should be able to fan cast these baits, retrieve them, fast, slow, erratic or in some cases, burn them back to the boat. Eventually you will find the one the fish prefer that day.

Top water baits will take a little longer to get the hang of at first. Some can change direction, some spit and others have a built in rattle in them. A prime area to try them is over weed tops, around lily pads and in the shaded areas over a sunken island.

When using a bait casting outfit you should be able to cover three different depths; top water, sub-surface and right on the bottom. Bass have the ability to take a bait effectively from almost any depth.

Two other high performance baits are the skirted jig and craw and a Slug-go. These baits perform very well in weed pockets, under catails and around stationary boats and low lying docks. You can spend a considerable amount of time using these baits "working" a shoreline.

To improve your hook set percentages, be sure to wait a second or two to allow the fish to close its mouth on the bait and take it down before you react to set your hook.

ANGLING FROM A CANOE (Fishing isolated areas and the shallows)

One of the best fishing vessels which I been using almost forever is a wide beamed, deep freeboard, triple keeled, fibreglass Algonquin canoe. I first found this canoe after looking high and low for that perfectly crafted to cover all of my needs kind of canoe. The above mentioned features had to be there. The wide beam is necessary for cargo area, a triple keel is for added balance and stability, a deep freeboard is for a smooth ride with very little resistance and fibreglass is very simple to repair if it gets a lot of abuse.

To complete the package I will also need three beavertailed paddles, the third being a back up if one breaks or is lost. In a canoe you should be using personal floatation devices (PFD'S). I would recommend two D.O.T. approved, an extra on to wrap your rods in when your on route and one for insurance.

When venturing out for a day of fishing you should only take the essentials. No more than two rods each, a bait caster and a spinning set to give you enough versatility for the day. Both angler's should pick a selection of preferred tackle and share one tackle box. With no motor you won't be going too far from the launch, so leave your lunches and cooler in your car parked in the shade. When you go back for lunch you will need to stretch and a rest before you head out for the remainder of the day.

The advantages of using a canoe are unlimited. Being able to fish in isolated lakes is always a bonus in most cases a very big bonus. You won't believe my fish stories. It's not too difficult to portage into some of those hard to get to lakes. The biggest bonus from an angler's point of view is the silent or natural approach.

As you enter a potential holding area, start your presentation with a lob cast and simply switch to a flippin' method when fishing the matted or weed choked areas. Continuing on to the pencil weeds, cattails and tall grassy areas to get closer to some ambushing bass or muskies.

Rather than anchor, you can stick a paddle in the mud and tie-off until the action dies down. When fishing from a canoe you can take full advantage of sight fishing to spot schools of bait fish, ripples of shallow running fish trying to elude your baits and locating underwater structure.

If you have a smooth running canoe you may consider installing a electric trolling motor to free up your hands. They have been known to run even quieter than with two paddling pals. I have even taken a depthfinder to act as my underwater eyes during an overcast day.

To get the most out of using a canoe and to protect yourselves from harm, stay away from bigger bodies of water and fast moving rivers. Consider land locked lakes and calm rivers, jeopardizing yourselves will only take the fun out of it. Never fish alone or after dusk.

If a motor boater passes by a little too fast and makes a wake. position your canoe with the bow into the oncoming wave, leave your paddles up and you can hop over it without a concern.

It's a good idea to practice with any new partners until you are confident in each others ability to steer and manoeuvre the canoe before heading out for a day.

PRIDE OF PRIVATE OWNERSHIP

Not everyone is as dedicated to the sport of fishing as I am. The decision is yours, based on the availability of what you would prefer to do with your valuable time.

After maintaining your house, garden and automobile, there isn't much time left to consider your family or friends.

Sturges boys, the next generation

Here is quote for what it's worth," Life is what you make it!" If you want something bad enough, you can always manage to get it.

Lets compare tools of the trade, a mechanic will insist on better quality tools to make his/her job a more rewarding one. A golfer may also play with a higher level of confidence if he/she plays with a good set of clubs. If a baseball player had premium equipment he/she would also play their game with confidence. Which brings us to fishing.

Similarly there is a variety of premium products on the market available for this sport. When choosing rods and reels, you have to consider a number of things such as, your level of dedication, and your skill level.

Like every sport, the more you play the easier the game. Your sincere desire to learn all you can about the sport through books, magazines, videos and watching televised fishing shows can help a lot. Getting out there and actually trying what you've learned to gain confidence is a must.

Some popular name fishing rods and reels to look for are Shimano, Daiwa, Berkley, Abu Garcia, Browning, Pinnacle, Mitchell, Zebco, Penn, Fenwick and St. Croix.

Each company has product which can be best suited for most skill levels.

If you manage to attend some of the many fishing show seminars, you may notice each Pro is representing their preferred brand of tackle by wearing a brand named monogrammed shirt, hat or by mentioning their preferences numerous times during the seminar.

Some things to look for when buying brand name products are, warranty service centres being close at hand.

An example of common problems are, replacing handles and bail springs. To get these replaced you would ordinarily have at least one month of down time, unless you asked, at point of sale, where the nearest "authorized repair dealer" was located. If you spend a little extra you may be eligible for a more realistic warranty for a longer period of time. Also some of the premium rod companies, offer a lifetime warranty. Look before you leap!

Something that will make life less stressful is, to keep the boxes your reel comes in for later reference. By loosening your drag system before you store them it will extend their life by not subjecting them to the dir and dust which could make them malfunction. A wise consumer knows, you will get quality if you pay for quality!

CUSTOM ROD BUILDING

Unless you get formal training on this art form, you will run into a number of stumbling blocks along the way. Again I'll mention that at every craft, practice makes perfect. In some cases, you may come to realize that it's out of your reach.

However, if you are one of the lucky ones, you should stay with it until you start getting orders within your circle of friends. If it develops into something better, you should be careful to keep control of it, instead of letting it get control of you.

A key element is to research to gain knowledge of suitable compo-nents, integrity of premium rod blanks, distances of line guides, reel seats and kits for making cork handles to get as close as you can to per fection. There are a number of very informative books on the market as well as at your local library.

When it becomes affordable, you can start stock piling the required components and accessories to begin. A large percentage of the preferred components can become available to you if you are able to search for it on the internet or check with your local fishing store or maybe read the ads at the back of some of the popular fishing magazines to find them.

One of the best ways to reduce your costs is to illuminate the middle-man and buy direct. To do this you'll probably have to register a company. Think of a catchy name that will describe exactly what you are doing and be sure to mention the word "custom" in it ie: Custom Rod Crafters, T.J.'s Custom Rod Builders or Premier Custom Rod Design. For the kind of money you will be having to charge you will soon be made aware that anglers will be expecting the very best components and accessories.

Although we are lead to believe that hand made products are made by hand, in the case of a good rod builder, he can buy a couple of tools to assist in making the job more bearable. One tool that is a must is a wrapping machine. With it you can roll it slowly with one hand while applying your winding thread. A thread bobbin can assist you in applying the winding uniformly.

Perhaps the most popular of specialty rods are "steelhead rods", ranging from eight feet to as long as thirteen feet; generally two pieces primarily designed for float fishing in our many beautiful streams. It seems that fly fishing has been growing in popularity all over. With this there has been an increased demand for custom built fly rods. They can come in different lengths as well as different weights. Some other requests may be for musky rods, ultra-light, walleye and bass rods.

The idea of owning a custom rod is it can be made to fit your hand or to suit your specific needs. It should come with a written lifetime guarantee. A masterpiece that can only be duplicated by the original builder. On a conventional store bought rod (mass produced), you'll be lucky to get more than a one year manufacturers warranty on any type of rod.

By comparison, a cork handled rod will prove to be much more sensitive, combined with a light weight (rod) blank made from high modulus graphite and complimented by wrapping low profile concept line guides, using the strongest rod winding thread and bonding materials to produce a fishing rod superior to anything you can find in the stores. It will be a masterful piece of equipment cherished for years to come.

To locate a reputable rod builder, you'll have to hunt around unless you are lucky enough to find one through your local fishing shop if they are an agent for one. Purchasing a custom built rod may never be of interest to you, unless, you are a truly devoted angling specialist who can appreciate the finer things that it can sometimes offer.

PRESENTATION

If you still believe all it takes to catch a fish is to cast out a popular lure several times and hope it is going to produce. I could only see that working on different species if the lure said C.I.L. wobbler on the side of it and you light it before it's tossed. All fish have striking similarities although they prefer natural presentations.

For example:

1) BASS will hit a top water lure if it tossed in front of them, twitched, then quick retrieved to a slow retrieve to provoke a strike.

2) WALLEYE will hit a deep diving minnow imitation lure if it passes through their strike zone. To effectively achieve this, your lures must dive in excess of 12 ft and continue to run at that depth.

3) TROUT on the other hand, will consistently take a roe bag if it is drifted down a stream under a Blackbird float. On many occasions trout will just open their mouths to take it, rather than bite it and run with it. (Unless there are other interested fish in the zone.

4) MUSKY & PIKE will viciously attack a bigger minnow or spinner if you make it look wounded. Do you know what a musky or a pike eat? What ever it sees that moves!

5) YOU ARE ALL FAMILIAR with a Texas and a Colorado, other effective methods of presentation that take trophy winning bass at tournaments all the time.

6) WALKING THE DOG with a Zara Spook, is another method that looks and acts like a wounded bait. Presented correctly this method can put fish in the boat all day long.

7) LIVE BAIT gently casted with only a single weedless hook can be a big producing rig by using frogs, worms, minnows, leeches and crayfish.

8) PITCHING a plastic worm under lily pads or under a cut bank laden with cat tails has won more bass tournaments than any other presentation out there.

9) DOWN-RIGGING a glow in the dark cut plug (J-PLUG &LYMAN) at around a hundred feet, with water depth of one hundred, ten feet or so. A method that has produced huge salmonoid on the Great Lakes.

10) SIDE PLANNING (planner boarding) is becoming more and more popular lately, and is effective on almost every gamefish. This is due to it being able to glide through the strike zones silently.

11) FLOAT TUBES are a fantastic approach. Jump in one, slip on the fins, enter the water and nothing can stop you as a versatile angler.

12) A METHOD THAT HAS PUT SEVERAL TROPHIES on my walls, is the split shot, slip sinker, floating jig head, presented on a drift using jelly and live baits. IT is a must try method.

13) FINESSING is a relatively new presentation, it is a top producing method among the tournament angler's. You can expect some major explosive action if presented under the right conditions. Slug-O is a great name brand to look for married with a 4 or 5/0 sized hook (offset).

14) FLY FISHING a form of an artful presentations combined with specific hand tied insect imitations. Practiced for years by mostly very dedicated angler's of all ages. A family tradition.

15) DIPSY DIVER a poor mans downrigger, can actually be adjusted to suit your desired depth. Can be very effective when fishing through a thermal clime, after a cold front has passed through.

Although I have not mentioned all the possible methods of presentations, a good number of these practiced while fishing your best bodies of water will boost your confidence as an angler.

You may have to consider purchasing a number of specialty rods, reels and equipment, as well as terminal tackle.

Be very cautious that you purchase from a reputable tackle outfitter. It will take up a lot of your time to become proficient at using all of them.

CONDITIONS OF FISHIN'

There is an infinite amount of conditions you may be faced with every time you head out to fish. Weather conditions can change constantly and dramatically throughout any given day as well as other determining factors.

WEATHER CONDITIONS: Wind speed and direction, water and air temperature, cloud cover/light penetration, barometric change (cold fronts), lunar influence (best time each month, full and new moon),

PRESENTATION FACTORS: water clarity/colour, spawning cycle (each species), seasonal temperatures, weed growth/location of food sources, abundance of natural forage, Ph factor (in water).

A comparison that I have witnessed is, the water colour of Georgian Bay compared to the Nottawasaga River. If I ventured out onto the bay, to fish for Rainbow trout, and used a specific lure and it performed in clear water, then I went and tried the same lure inland and fished from the shore in murky water, it would probably be futile in catching any fish because the conditions were dramatically different. Such as current, water clarity, water temperature, reduced wind speed, water depth, feeding areas are reduced and to become successful you would have to change your methods of presentation.

If it was the spring of the year, you would have the advantages of post spawn conditions, high water, increased population of fish, emerging insects and aquatic life and increased fishing pressure. The run generally lasts less than a week, although if Mother Nature isn't cooperating by bringing warmer weather, then it could be interrupted or delayed. Trout season starts the last Saturday in April in most areas.

Walleye and Northern pike open the weekend before May 24th, although you might find due to the effects of spawning (not schooled up) it could delay better fishing conditions until the latter part of May to the early part of June.

As the water begins to warm you will see the emergence of crayfish, leeches, weed growth and other aquatic life to bring bait fish closer to the shorelines, which will promote bigger fish to feed in these areas.

Bass and muskies are quite particular about the warming trends of water as they prefer to wait until the middle of June or later depending on the water temperatures near the shore before they begin nesting there. After the water warms up and they finish spawning you should be able to catch them consistently until the late fall. Musky feed aggressively until ice up in the late fall. This creates some of the best fishing conditions for trophy sized fish of the season. See you out there!

HANDLING FISH WITH CARE

One of our most valuable natural resource has to be our wildlife. Can you picture a forest with no wildlife or a body of water with the absence of birds or aquatic life? NO!

Then it would be wise if we could do something voluntarily to promote the populations of fish, so they would remain healthy and strong enough to sustain or even increase their current numbers.

By being careful when handling fish and releasing what you don't intend to eat in the same day could be beneficial to both you and our future generations, our children.

Here are some points to remember:

1) You shouldn't remove big fish from the water for long periods of time.Tail the fish when lifting, cradling it with your other hand under its mid-section.

2) Always remember to wet your hands to avoid burning the fish.Our body temperature is 98 degrees fahrenheit, compared to fish's body temperature which cold be as cold as 40 degrees.

3) Avoid over handling a fish, as you could remove much of its protective slime, which can be very harmful to its mortality.You will inevitably kill any fish if you keep them out of the water for an extended period of time

4) When releasing your fish, torpedo (dropping it into the water headfirst) it into the water to give it burst of air, provided you release it immediately. Otherwise, practice a gentle release the fish can generally let you know when its ready by swimming away on its own.

5) Avoid using a net if there is more than one treble hook being used. Too many anglers are forced to take far to long when untangling their lures from nets, which could result in killing a fish.

6) Bring your fish as soon as possible to avoid exhausting them. This will allow them to recover much sooner.

7) Remove all hooks by using a pair of needle-nose pliers to avoid unnecessary damage to the mouth and gill areas.For deeply hooked fish, you can cut your line and leave the hook in the fish as it will dissolve in a couple of days or keep the injured fish and include it in your daily limit.

8) Stay well away from a fish's gills and gill plates when removing hooks. Any damage to these areas will result in almost certain death.

9) By using proper sized hooks you can avoid injuring many smaller fish.

10) The use of gaffs and billy stick (clubs) is not necessary. If you aren't familiar with a species remove the hooks in the water. Fishing with the same partner constantly can assist in helping you fish like a team. Keep a camera handy so you can take your picture right away, then immediately return your trophy to the water.

ALL THE WHILE, VERSATILE (in-line spinners)

On a recent trip with Eric Warren the President of Double Loon, a Canadian manufacturer (Toronto, Ont.) of premium quality in-line spinners give me the opportunity to field test some proto-types on different species of gamefish.

With several decades of gamefishing experience, I am not afraid to admit that you can still teach this "old dog" new tricks! To begin with Double Loon has the largest selection of in -line spinners suitable for virtually every species of freshwater gamefish, every size imaginable, infinite colours, a hydra -dynamic body and quality finished blades sets them above the rest. To achieve optimum performance and to avoid

Ohhh Yeah! happiness IS a herd of Steelheads

extensive line twist always use a good quality ball bearing barrel swivel in black or stainless steel. (The smaller the better! #1 size) Warren's preferred methods for presentation is to not spend too long experimenting with any given colour. If you don't catch anything in five minutes, change the colour and maybe even the sizes until you hit the best producer.

Our first offering was for speckled trout also known as brook trout. Realizing that the average size of brook trout is around nine to ten inches, we used # 1 and # 2 blade sizes in silver and gold. Note:

smaller hooks fit into tiny mouths = higher productivity! Generally you would be looking for Brook trout in small streams or rivers, although I had guided my new found friend into an isolated deep lake that only has Brook trout in it.We agreed that our initial approach should cover as much area as possible by fan-casting all around structured areas of deeper water a short distance from the shoreline. It was an off day so we really had to work it. After having lots of fun we headed out for some lunch and then we continued to another lake to try our hand at walleye and smallmouth bass. On this new lake we worked it the same as for trout, although we could increase the lure size to # 3 and # 4 and change colour again. A simple countdown after your lure reaches your target can increase the probability of more strikes. An example of this is to cast, then start counting as soon as the lure touches water. If the water depth is eight feet you would count to six. This should start your retrieve at about two feet from bottom or more descriptive, in the strike zone. By adding a little repetitive tip action and frequently changing your speed you are creating an injured minnow action which will further improve the odds.

An effective method for trolling for deeper trout with these spinners, is to tie on a beaded keel weight sinker (1/8 to a 1/2 oz) your main line and add a two foot leader line (in metric that's both feet) of mono or copolymer. Then tie on your barrel swivel and attach your spinner. By casting it thirty to forty feet out behind the boat it should run less than a foot up from the bottom.

When trying this method for the first time you can determine the running depth by sending your line out slowly and monitor the action at your rod tip. If you bring up weeds, reduce your sinker weight, reduce the lure size or move to deeper water by moving further away from shore.

You may find that your favorite spinning rod and reel combination will be best suited when using in–line spinners in sizes #2 to #5 anything smaller ultra-lite gear is your best bet.

BEST BAIT FOR WALLEYE

DEW WORMS: Eight out of ten. Walleye anglers prefer to fish with Dew worms and Minnows. The remaining twenty percent are catching their Walleye on other baits.

RIBBON LEECHES: Presented on a Carolina type rig, replacing the bullet weight (sinker) with a Walking Sinker 1/8 or 1/4 ounce. Run the sinker up your line attached a B or BB sized split shot sinker at about the eighteen inch point (bite it with your teeth, no pliers). Choose a #8 or #10 wide gap hook in bronze or black. Cast out about thirty feet of line then begin drifting your bait. (Hooked once through the sucker end of the leech.)

CRANK BAITS: ie. Wally Diver, Fat Rap, Risto Rap or an Excalibur, Fat Free Shad. Pick specific areas that become deep off a shallow flat or deep weed line. Cast your bait at angles that will run only in the black (dark) water. Upon feeling a strike, sweep set the hook to pierce the fish's mouth.

JIG HEADS & GRUBS: Brightly coloured bodies are a major plus when fishing deep water 15 to 22 feet on a bright day or 10 to 18 on a cloudy day - Cast your bait to a promising location, allow it to touch bottom. Then hop it back to about half way then retrieve it the rest of the way at about half speed.

TUBE JIGS: (Scented or Salted): Ideally with a 1/4 ounce tube jighead, 3 or 4 inch long is good tube body.With this presentation imitating crayfish, select colours that are close to a natural colour. Cast to a potential productive area, allow the jig to touch the bottom, lifting and pausing all the way back to your rod tip try twitching it and pausing. This action simulates a burrowing crayfish. If a Walleye sees it he will most certainly take it.

JIGS AND PLASTIC MINNOWS: (colours natural, pearl or yellow). Walleye prefer to hug the bottom. Several reasons, they are sensitive to light, as a predator the bottom has been a Walleye's most effective attack point.

For this reason, rather than jig the particular bait you can swim it back stop and go.

BOTTOM WALKER: (1 ounce) With a three foot leader (clear mono line 10 lb test) With a single bladed tandem hook rig (Walleye worm rig) troll or drift this combination all day long.

FOOTBALL JIG: With a skirted twin tail grub. To effectively present this type of bait you must drag it rather than jig it or hop it. An ideal bottom condition is gravel or rock, with a gradual depth increase. It can also be pitched and flipped during overcast conditions.

SIMPLIFY WALLEYE

Some important things to remember when pursuing Walleye are that they habitually hug the bottom or keep to the shade because they have larger than average sized eyes which makes them sensitive to bright sunlight. The degree of sunlight will dictate their depth locations in conjunction with water clarity.

DIRECT SUNLIGHT: On a calm day (no breeze) you should be looking in water depths of around 18 to 22 feet. Good Clarity.

STEADY BREEZE: If a breeze creates a consistent ripple on the water surface, Walleye can be found moving up to depths near 14 to 16 feet of water.

SHADED AREAS: Walleye will remain in darkened areas of a lake if it is generally deeper than 16 feet provided there is an abundance of their preferred food choices. Bait fish, crayfish or leeches emerging from a sand bottom.

DRAMATIC DROP OFFS: If you can find an underwater shelf with approximate depths of 6 to 8 feet dropping into 18 to 20 feet you will have located a "Honey Hole".

WEED EDGES: Walleye will occasionally set themselves up to ambush bait fish if they are prevalent to an area. Although in must be at least 14 to 16 feet deep.

Happy
Walleye guy

OVERCAST CONDITIONS: For ardent Walleye anglers this is considered to be an excellent time to be fishing for Walleye as the tend to feed aggressively for most of the day rather than early morning or evening. Referred to as a low light condition.

YOUR LIVE BAIT CHOICES SHOULD INCLUDE, MINNOWS, LEECHES OR DEW WORMS.

MINNOWS: The minnows that out-perform the rest are, Emerald Shiners in the four to six inch range. Probably because they have prominent eyes and are more visible in low light conditions.

LEECHES: Probably the most durable of live baits, you can sometimes catch as many as three fish before you lose it.

DEW WORMS: Still the preferred bait of choice. Bigger is Better!

FALL MUSKY TACTICS

My latest adventure on one of the may beautiful lakes in the Haliburton Highlands took place in mid-November shortly before ice-up. The excitement level was increased as my two guests were the producer and the cameraman from the "Ultimate Fishing Show". This puts the pressure on me to perform with intentions of actually making constant connection with above average sized Muskies. D&M Custom Rods my current rod sponsor had supplied me with three speciality Musky rods. A six foot medium fast, bait casting rod, a five foot six trolling rod and a five foot-ten jerk bait rod. Each equipped with a premium reel (baitcasting) from Shimano filled with "Spiderwire" 6/30 6 pound diameter 30# test) and Super Silver Thread 20# test.

We began with a personally selected bait, mine was a hand crafted Lynx bucktail spinner in brass, yellow and chartreuse in a #7 blade. My partner felt his choice would preform because he had good luck with his "Sledge" Jerk-bait on other lakes. Before we started the camera, I had suggested using a relatively new scent on the market called "Kick n' Bass. To avoid soiling painted baits you should apply copious amounts of garlic based scent to the treble hooks. On a bucktailed spinner you can concentrate on the "dressed" part of the bucktail covering the hook. Most Muskie fishermen prefer to troll, however, my choice is to cast long to drop off areas. We began in an area of the lake which had a small river coming into it which is a feeding area for almost every kind of fish. The key is to locate the feeding fish and then concentrate on the area by fan casting using a fast retrieve to provoke an attack.

My first few casts were directed on an area that was close to shore. With no results, our strategy changed to casting in deeper water, where the water appeared black. By casting in to these darkened areas and hesitating for about ten seconds to allow the bait sink out of view, then retrieve it quickly, could in a sense, pull them out of their hole. About my fourth cast I watched a long musky follow my bait, called a follow up. Once I spotted it my speed of retrieve was reduced to slow and then this big brute torpedoed ahead and viciously devoured the bait.

Normally you may have had to perform a "figure eight" to trigger a strike. I am convinced that this fish was attracted to my bait because it was leaving a scent trail, Kickn'Bass (Garlic). We switched baits about an hour later in which time we caught four good sized Muskies, although the action was slowing down. We tried a Believer attached to the deeper diving eye to get it into the strike zone and my fishing partner switched to a jointed "Sledge". We had a few takes although we could not connect.

After completely covering the area, we agreed to explore other parts of the lake to see if we could stimulate a few more strikes with the Buck-tailed Spinner. Generally it can take up to one hundred casts to connect with a single fish. In late fall the population of Muskies are feeding more aggressively in an effort to fatten up for the long winter ahead. As long as you can get into their "Strike Zone" you should be able to con-sistently produce.

Next year, do not be in a hurry to put your boat away for the winter. Invite a few friends to join you in some explosive action for Muskies of the North. When you fish this time of the year, you could virtually "own the lake".

BIG BAITS FOR BIG FISH ?

Fall fishing has been an ongoing passion of mine for some time. It adds to the excitement during deer hunt week , with sundays being closed to hunting we can spend the entire day in search of some "husky muskies". For the past several years I have either fished with a friend or taped television fishing shows.

Provided the lake hasn't "flipped" (upper and lower levels of lake cool to nearly the same temperature) or froze over by this time, fishing should still be good. Muskies at this time of the year have a relentless appetite at which time they feed on most anything that moves through their strike zone in order to fatten up for winter. The weather is quite unpredictable from about the middle of September through to end of the season (Nov. 30). The thing I like about this time of the year is, reduced boat traffic, virtually no cottagers and no fishing pressure. You might say "You own the lake "!

Our "big bait"tackle selection will include Rapala's, Husky Jerk baits, Smithwick's, Rattlin'Rouges (suspending), Jointed Believers and Slug-Go's as our artificial presentations and our live bait would be six inch Emerald Shiners.

It is often said that it can take as much as one hundred hours to catch one musky. I'm sure this comment was based on fishing larger bodies of water. Fortunately my time is spent on pristine lakes throughout the Haliburton Highlands in central Ontario. These lakes are smaller land locked or isolated lakes that are dominated by above average sized muskies.

By choosing high performance innovative, well defined minnow imitating body baits such as the fore mentioned and the introduction of game fish scents, you too will increase your odds. If you are fishing this late in the season you will in pursuit of musky and commonly hook into walleye over five pounds. Both these fish change their feeding habits from foraging on schools of bait fish to independently cruising for single fish in half to three pound range and in some cases they will cannibalize their own.

We started by heading for a quiet deep bay where a stream flowed into it. This is an ideal location because as the days cool bait fish will return to the lakes and remain there until the spring. This brings a good population of muskies to the area to feed, so we use the imitation the closely resembles the indigenous bait fish. Creek chub are black with a white belly which is very close in colour to the our Husky Jerks. First cast the lure past the area you want to retrieve your bait through to avoid spooking the fish and to achieve your most natural presentation using a wounded minnow action, stop and go. About five seconds into the retrieve I felt a vicious strike, I leaned back on my rod and up out of the water comes a ten pound musky, head shaking, torpedoing and bull dogging frantically in an effort to break free. After a couple of minutes the fish excepted defeat. I leaned over and grabbed it in the notch above its gill plates, unhooked my lure and gently returned it to the dark water.

5 Big guys

Our next action was a "follow up", it was at least in the forty inch range, I slowed down my retrieve and tried doing a figure eight to provoke a strike. This is common practice as a last effort although it doesn't always work. I like to switch to another rod rigged differently, cast in the direction the fish was headed and retrieve the bait slowly. Also I prefer casting to deep dark holes rather than troll for them.

Next year don't be in a hurry to put away your boat or your fishing rods. Instead call a friend and explain that they are going to miss the best time of the year to fish if they pass on this opportunity.

CHAPTER THREE
Trout Tactics

A "real" "Jig-Head" fisherman!

ANGLER'S ETIQUETTE WHEN STREAM FISHING

After a very long winter I was feeling a little "cabin feverish", so I called up a friend who hadn't tried fishing for Rainbow trout from the shore in his lifetime. Chris bought us a coffee and a muffin, and we were off to Craigleith to test the water. We were not dealing with very promising fishing conditions. After about a dozen long casts we concluded this was not the place to "work", so "Hi-Ho, Hi-Ho," it's off to Meaford we go! This is an old stomping ground of mine, although it has changed dramatically since I last visited. It now has a lot more water to cover, with an abundance of room to choose the techniques that may be best suited to the conditions.

Shortly after our arrival, we began fan casting from shore using a couple of select lures at about the halfway point of the river. Some other options would come about when someone catches a fish. I watch to see what's working and either match it exactly or use something similar.

We were dealing with below normal temperatures, with a brisk on-shore breeze that demanded every layer of clothes we had on. Although we remained fairly optimistic for the first hour or so, the cold was making it very difficult to persevere.

We netted two fish in the first half hour, one frying pan sized and the other spawning size, which was skillfully returned unharmed. Neither were caught by my friend or myself.

It seemed that spawn sacks were the performing bait choice of the morning. Bottom bouncing was the producing presentation, the cold had effected their aggressiveness to a slow take.

The excitement began when I noticed a gentleman holding his noodle rod at about his shoulder height with a "what do I do now that I have hooked this fish and I have forgotten my net?" —look on his face. Without hesitation I called over, "Do you need a net?" He replied,

"Yeah! It would help a lot." After lending a hand we shared some small talk about where he was from and how many he managed to hook.

A few minutes later I heard a loud splash behind us. It was a better trout breaking water fighting with an angler to break free. It was another fisherman that had neglected to bring a landing net along. Within seconds we had the brute subdued and in the net. It was over seven pounds, an impressive male, and muscular. This fellow was an experienced angler, not only did I not spot him hiding, I didn't hear him until the fish broke water. As the fish entered the net he told me to shake him loose, he was just having fun today. I complimented him and he thanked me for my efforts.

Opening day wasn't far off, the crowds of visitors would be limiting our space to a shoulder to shoulder situation and conditions could be less than comfortable then.

It doesn't take any time away from your fishing to generously assist a fellow angler in netting their fish and if you notice that someone close to you has just hooked one, have the courtesy to reel in and make room. Fishing is supposed to be fun, it makes for a better day for all of us.

HIGH-WATER EXCITEMENT (Early Spring Rainbow Trout Fishing)

As a sports fisherman for over four decades, I have been able to experience some real breathtaking and explosive one on ones with just about every species of game fish. By comparison, rainbow trout are by far the toughest to reckon with.

If you took the time to do a random specific species survey, you would likely discover that about 40% of anglers are ardent rainbow trout (Steelheaders) enthusiasts. To achieve proficiency at catching these fish, it is of utmost importance for an angler to be knowledgeable of the rainbows seasonal movements, their food preferences and where they are most likely to be located in the natural habitat. In knowing this, you can choose your specialty tackle and equipment. Like most species of sportfish you can pursue rainbow with quite a selection of methods and techniques.

Noodle rods married with either a float reel or a premium quality spinning reel with a high line capacity is a very popular choice of many for the stream approach. Another alternative is downrigging from your personal water craft or contracting a charter boat using gear such as levelwind trolling reels on heavier duty rods. Not to forget fly fishing equipment.

By the opener in late April, you will find hundreds of anxious "Steelheaders" dotting the shorelines near the river and stream mouths throughout the Georgian Triangle Area. Whether you primarily fish for food or for the sport of it, –we will all be anticipating that our presentation can stimulate that long awaited powerful strike.

When a rainbow takes your drifted baits, such as a spawn sac or stone fly, you will be able to detect even the slightest interruption,

followed by a timed hook set. Immediately upon setting the hook, you will put a death grip on your rod. Your fish will proceed by attempting to strip you of as much line as it possibly can. Followed by bulleting out of the water to gain enough slack to escape. If it is unsuccessful at first,the second try could be a series of head shakes escalating into tail walking. As it tires, your fish may resort to rolling itself in your fishing line with hopes that this stunt can set it free. By this time you may both be winded. The rainbows final efforts will be to take you into an area to try to snag you up. It will by now be convinced that it has been defeated. You win!

The Ontario Ministry of Natural Resources constantly adds amendments to trout regulations. Before venturing out, get yourself a copy and read them carefully. I understand they have been introduced to promote natural propagation so this fierce fighting species can remain plentiful in our district. Finally!

FISHERMEN'S EXCUSES

When we all began fishing there was only three pieces of tackle we needed to catch a fish—hook, line and a sinker combined with some bait. Nowadays it's become much more scientific due to modified presentations, the aid of electronics, increased knowledge of fish habitat and the use of topographical or hydrographical maps.

We are steadily improving as anglers by selecting specialty rods, reels and tackle. Fish habitually feed twice a day, early in the morning for several hours and again in early to late evening under ideal weather conditions.

These feeding trends however may be disrupted by a number of climactic changes such as air temperature, cloud cover, penetration of light and the barometric pressure. In addition to this, there is the water temperature, water clarity, wind speed and direction. Primary factors commonly overlooked are the consistency of the weather and the lunar influence. Better fishing during a full moon and a new moon.

Once we learn to realize the effects of these conditions, we can find a lot of the missing pieces from the puzzle. When the weather changes you will be forced to change your presentations to suit the conditions. In a lot of cases you may find that changes actually improve your chances by creating ideal conditions.

Several examples such as reduced wind speed, may give you a better drift and allow you to have improved boat control. Cloud cover will allow the fish to move up to feed closer to shore. A good warm rain shower can improve your day by adding oxygen to the water. It will make the fish feed more aggressively and would give certain fish the opportunity to move out of a shallow area. On a warm summers day the rain forces insects into the water where they will soon be consumed by top feeding fish.

Cold fronts dramatically change fish feeding habits by shocking the fish enough so they won't feed for about a day or so. In these cases you will have to slow down your presentation to trigger a strike.

With this information you can tell your curious friends the reason you didn't catch very many fish was due to a number of scientific reasons above their comprehension, rather than quickly fabricate your own excuses, which may have been used before.

For me, lunar influence has been a hard sell, but only until I get a chance to take that person fishing later in the month to prove my point. Again, three days of consistent weather is the "KEY" to most of the conditions.

NO EXCUSES

I'm sure we all have at least one depressing story about, "The big fish that got away". In most cases, it could be related to some sort of human error. Whether it was or not, the excuses will be too weak to even convince a fool.If I can come to the rescue with several proven suggestions and solve many of the simple anglers mistakes which happen often, then read on.

I have seen many people hook into a big fish and almost immediately they become so excited that they are compelled to fall into a state of panic. Once this occurs, you may find yourself applying unnecessary pressure and a tendency to horse the fish, which results in a break-off. If you manage to get the fish to the side of the boat safely, then you'll want to go all the way and try lifting the fish out of the water. If you reach this point you will break off for sure.

Another couple of situations are created by failing to adjust the drag on your reel properly and not using a proven knot to tie on your lure and hooks. I recommend either the improved clinch knot (Berkley) or the polymer knot. Both should be moistened (with saliva) before being tightened to reach their optimum performance level.

A sad mistake I have witnessed occasionally is seeing someone pinch on their split shot sinkers using pliers, instead of using their teeth. They are designed to be attached by less aggressive methods to avoid the chance of cutting part way through the line and reduce the line strength dramatically.

An acquaintance of mine loses eight out of ten of his hooked fish by failing to position his rod at the one o'clock position to act as a shock absorber. Rather than just reel the fish in, you could angle it in and be able to utilize your drag system as well as the flex in your rod.

After catching a couple of scrappy fish, be sure to check for line abrasion and trim off a couple of feet and re-tie if you notice any line damage.

If you become the net person, be sure to wait until your partner gives you the okay. Then precede by netting the fish carefully by the "head" only. Proper handling of your fish is of utmost importance. Carelessness can result in a reduced mortality rate. Particular caution should be the order of the day when handling the toothy characters, walleye, pike and muskie.

Rule of thumb is, trout and salmon should be beached while fishing streams and if you are fishing open water, you can tail them by supporting their belly. With bass, pinch their bottom lip between your thumb and your four fingers and lift. With walleye, you can push down its dorsal fin to wrap your hand around its back and lift. If you must remove pike or musky from the water, then position your hand across its back just behind the gill plates (the notch) and grip the tail for extra stability.

All game fish should be played smoothly and as quickly as possible, admired (take a picture) then returned right away. Ride 'em, release 'em and let someone else enjoy the excitement another day.

EARLY SEASON TROUT

For a number of reasons I can't often plan to fish for Lake Trout in the Spring of every year, probably because you will find me preparing for Rainbow stream-fishing or Speckled Trout fishing. With the fact that we live on, ten minutes away from some of Ontario's best Trout fishing areas.

This year a couple of angling friends and I are planning a versatile fisherman's weekend in late May. We will be trying our hand at Lake Trout, Walleye, and stream Brook Trout just after the season opens "Ice Out".

Our approach for Lake Trout will be first fish the past Spawn areas close to shore. Although consideration will be given to areas of out going streams or river mouths as they generally have a good concentration of minnows returning to their summer residences in the upper reaches and throughout the water shed. Here Minnow imitations or live Minnows will be the order of the day. Smaller spoons, in-line spinners, Rapala's A.C. Shiners and jig and grub presentations will produce the best.

In cooler water a slower retrieve would be advised although if you are experiencing a warming trend these trout will hit more aggressively.

Rainbow Trout share same waters as Speckled Trout and generally will be looking for emerging or flying insects to stimulate their feeding trends. Loose eggs are prevalent throughout the migrating trail as far up as the head waters.

In the case of Speckled Trout, you can tempt this species by downsizing your presentation to 0 to 1 sized in-line (brightly coloured) spinners, single egged hooks in as tiny, a size #12 or #14 egg hooks or use a earth or red worm on a bronze or black premium hook in the same sizes. In a faster current condition you might consider installing a split shot with enough weight to allow it to bounce on the bottom.

With any trout, you should always be careful not to cast a shadow on the area you are planning to fish as they 'spook' easily and will "not" feed when disrupted in their normal environment. Longer gentle casts towards the middle of the stream and allowed to drift with the current will be more productive.

My approach has always been from meandering slowly up stream with methodical casts to deeper colder holes that can provide a good quantity of oxygenated (cold) water as well as source of floating food choices and cover.

Babbling brooks and streams become an endless trail for ardent fly fishers who's presentation are based on replicating the natural emerging aquatic life such as nymphs, larvae and flying insects placed evenly like an artists brush stroke. I have always applauded fly fishers as they generally recycle and reuse or natural resources by using fine 'barbless' hooks and a wet hand to avoid unnecessary injury to our many Trout species.

In mentioning three different species of trout we can talk all day on specific tackle selection to improve as a versatile angler.

STREAM FISHING WITH ARTIFICIAL BAIT

My most recent experiences while fishing streams running into larger bodies of water using artificial only have been extremely rewarding. In the past fishing the southern watersheds such as the Credit River mouth and the Ganaraska River, have brought me bountiful amounts of salmon and trout using popular lures like, Little Cleos, Krocodiles, #2 Mepps and Panther Martin's. However, the Nottawasaga River tends to always run faster and is more commonly deeper. For these reasons, both species are able to pass through the lower reaches of the mouth due to ideal unobstructed high water. Under these conditions your presentation must provoke a strike rather than imitate a food source. The fish seem to prefer an erratic action such as a flatfish or a rattlin' spot with a prominent eye in fluorescent orange or a chartreuse colour in a minnow imitation. We are dealing with reduced visibility in a lot of cases caused by rainfall, erosion and quick moving water. If the water clarity improves, so will the effectiveness of your lures.

It is imperative to cast above the high percentage areas to introduce your bait using the speed of the current as an aid to avoid spooking the fish. You are attempting to introduce your bait in the most natural way possible to provoke a wild and vicious strike. To achieve desirable

depths, utilize light monofilament fishing line (Berkley Trilene) or a micro diameter copolymer line (Super Silver Thread) in 6 or 8# test.

Consider using a longer medium action rod ranging from seven feet to 10 ft. 6 when tangling with brutes. Use the bend in the rod as a shock absorber and be careful in setting the reel drag to avoid break-offs.

In early spring as the water gradually warms, the emerging aquatic life will stimulate fish to feed more readily. During this phase of spawning run will get most stream fishers to go to conventional baits such as roe sacks, worms and spinners. In my case, I will switch to 1/8 oz. jigheads with prism eyes, dressed with curly tailed grubs. Some preferred colour combinations are yellow head or pink head with a white grub or red and silver head with a black grub.

One of the most effective methods of presentation is to cast gently upstream, allow the jig to make contact with the bottom. Each instant you feel bottom, lift it up so it will make its way to well below you. Then bring it back and cast to another spot and keep repeating this until you detect a strike. By using your chest waders, you should be able to cover areas more thoroughly. Key in on the deeper holding pools and in the eddies behind boulders. Concentrate on the obvious deeper zones to avoid getting snagged constantly. You should expect a strike immediately, although don't get stuck on a colour that isn't performing. Change your bait to change your luck!

SPRING LAKERS

Lake Trout as been widely protected in the last several years, mainly due to the declining population caused by increased fishing pressure. In an attempt to increase the population we were given the Splake (Speckle and Lake Trout Cross). Their mortality rate was good although they are not capable of reproduction.

To catch some scrappy Lake Trout all you will need is fresh fishing line and a colourful assortment of spoons such as a Little Cleo,

William's Wabler, Krocodiles, Blue Fox's Pixie spoon, Eppinger's 5 of Diamonds or a Crippled Herring (Jigging lure).

Shortly after ice out Lake Trout will come up from the depths to participate in a frenzy of feeding on primary smelts. Although any type of bait fish can become lunch, for this reason it is wise to use Minnow imitation lures. When looking for Lake Trout concentrate on feeder creeks which run into the lakes and these areas are where you will locate smelts migrating up stream for their annual spawning run.

If a Trout sees you it will not strike due to the shock of your presence (you'll spook them) stay well back and begin fan casting from your anchored boat. Each time you completely cover a feeder creek area, move your boat in about 30 feet and do it again. The depth range is not as important as the water temperature. If you are fishing during a warm Spring day Lake Trout will have moved out to deeper colder water. Lake Trout will only remain in the shallows until the Smelt run is over or until the water temperature is above 55f. Your method of fishing will have to change from flat lining (trolling without downriggers) to fishing at a fixed depth (downrigger baits) When you are forced to change methods you are advised to increase your line strength, your lure sizes and change to heavier equipment.To locate fish use a sonar, look for bait fish, most likely there will be feeding Trout close by.

Set your down riggers at a depth that runs just above the Trout. To successfully take a Minnow, Trout prefer to attach from the blind spot (behind from the underside) to avoid having to chase a Minnow. Another method for catching Lake Trout in early Spring is to put an Emerald Shiner (3") under a slip float, set the float to depth that runs about six inches up from the bottom. Cast into the current of the feeder creek and watch for it to disappear.

A RARE AND UNIQUE DISCOVERY

Generally, most of our fishing rod manufacturers mass-produce "their" rods to suit the industry's following. In other words they are assembled very much the same by using generic blanks and components. It's common knowledge that their reasoning is based on volume, price and market demand. Unless we venture out to locate alternative rod manufactures we will be limited to using an only average product.

As we advance as anglers, we will always be looking for better quality equipment. After numerous disappointments, I now insist on premier quality fishing rods and reels. Fortunately my needs have been reached and surpassed by D&M Fishing Rods. A Canadian manufacturer owned and operated by Master rod builder Ian Duffield. D&M Rods are an internationally recognized company their Canadian market has experienced tremendous growth in sales in the last year especially.

D&M offers a rare and unique top quality fishing rod, an instrument. They have assembled a team of professional rod builders capable of producing virtually every type of specialty fishing rod possible. Constructed using only the finest quality rod blanks, components and their exclusively designed reel seats machined from Rosewood and Ebony. All of their rods are built to perfection! It's great feeling to be able to tell your friends that you'll "get what you paid for, for a change".

Traditional anglers will be extremely impressed by D&M's wide selection of specialty rods, for Steelhead (noodle/float), fly, walleye, bass and musky. They are also extremely proud of their new improved Float Reels which are available in a 4 1/2" diameter (centre pin) precision anodized aluminum reel that pays out effortlessly and comes in clear, gold, black and the new metallic gun metal grey.

To receive your free product catalogue from D&M Rods: Phone (519) 853-5081 email: dmrods@globalserve.net www.dmrod.com.

IN-VESTED TACKLE (Stream Fishing Essentials)

If you are as dedicated to each species of sportfish as I am, then you probably also have quite a collection of tackle and equipment for this seasons rainbow trout run.

Generally when considering fishing for rainbow, even before wetting a line, I'll be buying up all the essentials to stuff my fishing vest pockets with specialty tackle such as assorted sizes of split shot sinkers, egg hooks in several styles and colours (gold, bronze & black). A variety of quilled featherlite floats such as Blackbirds, Carousel or Thills. For insurance a package of wet flies such as black stoneflies and another of egg sucking leech flies. An assortment of in-line spinners, specifically Mepps, Blue Fox and Panther Martin's ranging from size one to size three.

If you are fishing an area that requires a longer cast it is best to fill another pocket with Little Cleo's and several duplicated colours such as blue and silver and green and chartreuse. And a couple of colours, pink prism and pearl white.

When using spinners and spoons you'll need to pack at least a dozen ball bearing, interlock" black" snap swivels in Size #0 or #1. The black reduces an unnatural appearance and reduces damaging line twist. Also it allows your lures to run unrestricted for optimum performance.

For the bottom bouncing method select two sizes of egg sinkers, 1/4 oz. and 1/2 oz. as well as a package of coloured styro-foam floaters to tie in to my egg sacs. I will also pack two empty film canisters with my wife's favourite, coloured miniature marshmallows, which work better than the floaters in faster currents.

As a precaution, I will pack a green garbage bag to carry a fish or two and to make a poor mans raincoat if the need arises. Also two empty bread bags to store fresh fish eggs in, if I manage to catch a hen (female trout). You can actually milk her into the bag until you have enough and then return the fish to the water to complete her spawning process.

After loading up my vest with tackle, there is still the other accessories to simplify the catch and release—a pair of pliers or haemostats for removing and straightening hooks. To trim spawn sacs and clip the tag off after tying on leaders and hooks I'll fasten a pair nail clippers to lanyard.

If the area isn't too covered with anglers I prefer to make most of my strategic presentations utilizing my chest waders.

Although this is my only my second season living in the area, I have had success in previous years as a tourist at Meaford, Craigleith and at the mouth of the Nottawasaga river. I am drawn back every year due to the endless challenges, the exceptional quality of rainbow trout that this vast area sports. Clean and Mean.

Don't be surprised if I accidentally rub shoulders with some of you, I'll be the guy wearing the big smile.

CHARTERING A BOAT

If you and your friends want to experience an exciting day of great fishing, you should consider renting (chartering) a boat on the Great Lakes. Close to home or just north of where you live, east or west can also be an option.

A big "misconception" is that you can only charter a boat for Salmon and the various species of Trout.

Lake Erie or Bay of Quinte have fantastic charters (guided trips) for Walleye from early May to as late as November. To locate some of the available charter services you can first ask around, drive to your preferred launch point or check with your favourite fishing magazine. For those who have home computers you can get this information through the Internet. Discuss the possibilities with your friends, family or co-workers. Determine a date, and with who, ask for half the cost up front and mention if you do not show you will lose your deposit. It amazing how everyone shows up.

Generally there is no reason to do price comparisons. Almost all of the charter boats for Salmonoids are the same price, Generally they (the charter skippers) will give you boat rental price for six (6) hours for a morning or an afternoon trip.

Although there are lots of charter boats available along the marine areas on the Great Lakes, you may have to look a little harder for guiding services and pay a little more for his expertise. What you want is someone who is able to put you on big fish consistently. Some days it just is not possible, if you are understanding of that you could have the right attitude before you leave shore. If you do catch a big fish, you will probably catch several.

When fishing with several friends or relatives, you may have to establish a rotating system. An example would be five (5) people fishing you all pick a card, highest card takes the first (strike) knock off. If the fish gets off you automatically, move to the next person, or you can say that the person who organized the trip can go first and turns come as you paid him.

Of course you may want to decide on a cash prize or buy lunch for the big fish of the day winner or think up your own prize.

Whatever you do, do not forget the camera and make sure everyone has a valid fishing license. Don't forget to tell your friends what a great time you had and show off your pictures, you may create enough of an interest that you will be arranging another fishing trip with a whole new set of friends.

SPECK-"TACULAR" FISHING

Speckled or brook trout (the same fish) are commonly overlooked because size seems to be important when fishing this species of gamefish. Of all our gamefish, speckled trout are the most colourful and the most difficult to catch. An average sized speckled trout is about nine inches long. A one pound fish is very rare; to catch one over five pounds is a catch of a lifetime. I'm still trying to break my own personal record of five pounds. I know exactly where to go for it, I just haven't been able to get there as of yet. Maybe this fall!

If you've ever considered these little beauties, it's best to down size your equipment to ultra-lite tackle and drastically reduce your hook sizes to a #12 or #14, if you intend to be successful. These fish are generally misunderstood; most anglers think that they can use conventional tackle and equipment. Although, common sense will tell us we won't be expecting extremely large fish, so light tackle will be our best choice.

A five foot six inch light action rod married with an ultra-lite spinning reel; then spooling it with four to six pound test mono or copolymer line should work excellent for anyone. If you are lucky enough to tie into a one pound speck, it will feel like a five pound fish. Speckled trout fight as aggressively as a smallmouth bass would of the same size range.

Trolling for specks should be the furthest thing from your mind as they hold primarily close to deep (cold) shorelines or throughout the deepest pools and under cut banks of rivers and streams.

Lure choices should include in-line spinners such as Mepps, Blue Fox, Lynx, Panther Martins or Double Loons in sizes ranging from "00" to size one blades. Panther Martins come in body weight sizes, the 1/32 to 1/4 ounce should perform very well as they have in the past for my clients. Brightly coloured lures tend to stimulate vicious attacks (yellow, pink, white and plain silver or gold).

With the fact that these fish spook very easily, I suggest that you always cast upstream and allow the spinner to drift with the current although you'll have to control it until it reaches the front of you. Then quickly retrieve it and repeat the motion. Move further up if you fail to get any strikes or until you find a tempting deep pool. If you find that the lure keeps coming to the surface, then you should slow down your retrieve.

These tiny baits are designed to imitate both aquatic life and minnows. Other baits to consider are scented micro tube jigs or grubs casted with and without a quill float. When rigging up with live bait, you can use earth worms (red worms) rather than dew worms, leeches, pin-head (tiny) emerald shiners and also small grasshoppers. Look for smaller black or bronze hooks because they are less obvious and they are less likely to spook these finicky fish.

If you really want to have a fantastic day of fishing, your day will be based on how quiet you can remain. If you ever fish from a boat, it is imperative that your presentation is as close to natural as possible. To achieve this, drift over the areas you are going to be fishing using only the speed of the wind. No anchor! You can easily spook these fish by driving over them with your motor boat. If you fish from the shore, be sure to stand well back from the shore so you don't cast a shadow on the water. Use gentle lob casts and you will achieve success more consistently.

Do not give a man a fish, but teach him how to fish

(THE JOYS OF) FISHIN' TRADITION

As a youngster I was first introduced to fishing with my four older brothers, mainly as a tag-along, I think, and later developed a genuine passion for the sport.

Our father felt confident enough in his angling ability to put food on the table for his family of nine. So Saturday would be our day for fish and chips. The times we didn't go, the days we couldn't catch any fish, quickly became "chip days". As we grew up the fishing team got smaller. Eventually I would find myself spending the time fishing only with my father. I'm not complaining though. It was great!

He would always say, "Betcha a buck that you won't catch a fish bigger then your old dad"! I think it was his way of paying me for pulling the dew worms the night before.

He'd always have a good joke to start the day off right. I could always count on him If he said we were going fishing he would be ready to go come rain or come shine.

I can remember a great time when we were invited to my uncle's cottage, up in the Haliburton Highlands, for the weekend. We arrived late on Friday evening with just enough time to plan Saturdays outing. My uncle, a dedicated worm fisherman, felt that if you wanted to catch bass you had to have huge dew worms.

The next morning we were up a the crack of dawn, with my uncle's " We will be having fish for breakfast", so let's get going.

We grabbed our gear, the worms and next thing you know, we were heading for a spot my Uncle called "stump cove." We came in slow and quiet. From that point on we could only whisper. What an excellent fishing spot it was. Most of the fish we caught were two and half pounds and a couple were over three pounds. It seemed like all I was doing was filling the stringer. After about half an hour the fish turned off. We had agreed earlier that there was another spot we were going to try. My Uncle said, "Lets go, and hurry!" Both men were WW II Navy veterans, so an order was to be carried out right away or sooner. So we

The author as a younger man; part of 3 generations of Canadian fishermen carrying on the fishin' tradition.

brought up our lines and I immediately started the motor and began to speed away. All of a sudden we heard a Clunkity Clunk. I turned off the motor, and looked over the transom to see our mess of fish being dragged towards the bottom by the liveliest fish.

My father asked "what was that ?" Then my uncle asked, "did you bring the stringer of fish in?" Ahh, Ahh? I replied "I'll get it". All that came up was half a chain and no fish, I knew I was in for a long lecture. As if I didn't have enough problems, there wasn't another bass caught the rest of the day.

You should have heard my aunt verbally abusing us for the rest of the weekend. From that day on I always pull up the stringer before starting the motor and I bring a camera to get proof of the big one.

With my three boys, I started them fishing at about three years of age. You can find us at our family's rod and gun cabin, from May 24th on. Early in October I was able to get away with my eldest son Matt for his first try at musky fishing. While trolling for musky we caught a couple of walleye's around six or seven pounds, and we have pictures to prove it. We will be spending a lot of time on the Nottawasaga River this spring, I think he is strong enough to tangle with some huge Rainbow trout. I'll be sure to take pictures.

Eric my youngest has been telling everyone that he will be going rainbow trout fishing with his big brothers and his dad when it's summer time.

It has gone to a vote and it's unanimous, the eighth annual father and son fishing derby is going to be held in the Wasaga Beach area in early spring. All for fun and fun for all!

The new generation of anglers. Alex and Eric (my son)

CHAPTER FOUR
Slick Ice Fishing Tricks

BRING YOUR CHUM FISHING (Ice Fishing Technique)

When ever you buy minnows, you'll lose a few on the way to your fishing destination. After spending money on them it seems a shame to just throw them away. What I do to use up the dead ones is, pop their air sack by squeezing their middle, then drop several of them in the water to CHUM the hole.

Drop them into the specific holes you will be using for live bait presentations. This technique will stimulate fish to feed by showering them with a handful of minnows. After their unhindered feeding frenzy, you can introduce your line rigged with live minnows. They won't even be suspicious of the presence of your hooks until you give it a real good tug to set it. Concentrate all your live bait fishing in the holes you've chummed. Because we are permitted to use two lines you may feel more comfortable if you chum only the holes outside your ice hut. While inside you can jig fish without getting tangled with the other angler's. Not being convinced that "spreaders"are the only way to fish live bait. You'll catch me practicing a method that produces better fish because it involves using bigger minnows, three to five inches long.

Realizing that fish move much slower (are lethargic) in colder water when taking live bait. You can use a presentation that allows your minnow to circle an area just off the bottom about twenty inches. To rig it use a 1/4 oz. slip sinker, with a size "B" split shot at the twenty inch mark. Then tie a #8 sized hook to the end of your fishing line. To install your minnow to the hook insert it through the nostril hole in the upper lip. This will allow the minnow to swim more lively and stay alive much longer because it's not injured and the hook doesn't interfere with it's gill function. My preferred choice of minnows when ice fishing is the emerald shiner. They have prominent eyes and their colours are more visible in the deeper waters. Dace and sucker minnows tend to hide on the bottom when fished individually. By allowing the shiner to swim freely up from the bottom, a striking fish attacks the bait from the underside just behind it's eye (blind spot) by inhaling it or mouthing it. What we are doing is creating an ideal strike situation for bigger feeding fish. Give this one a try, and don't forget your chum!

CRUSHED ICE & FISH TALES

I was having a conversation recently with two fishing acquaintances of mine who told me how they had resolved an access problem they were faced with while fishing late in the season. Both of these guys simply don't know when to quit!

Upon arriving at their favourite fishing hole, they were faced with a fresh layer of thin ice which would have deterred anyone else, but not these guys. They turned and looked at one another, then they began shot-putting boulders in the direction they intended to fish. After making entry holes through the ice, they rigged up and started casting to the holes. Once in, they jigged their artificial bait to imitate a bottom feeding action. It wasn't long before they made contact. Normally they would simply retrieve the fish and beach it (play it up onto the shore). With the ice hinders this they were forced to play the fish to just below the surface and horse the fish so it would actually jump out of the hole and land on the ice. Due to the autumn chill the had to bring the fish back to in front of them quick enough so it would not freeze on the ice.

Typically most people would be hanging up their rods in early September, although some of my biggest fish were caught in September through to the end of November as our season remains open in most of Central Ontario until then for both Walleye And Musky. That's three months of prime-time fishing excitement! Here are some of my true Fish Tales during this time of the year!

One weekend after deer hunting (early November) a couple of my clients had prearranged to rendezvous with me on a favourite lake which holds some of the largest Walleye for miles around. We started off with having to deal with some very cold severe winds which seem to limit our presentations to heavier jigs. We decided to cut our day short for safety reasons and due to the less than desirable fishing conditions. It appeared that the lake had "flipped". This is where the water temperature at the top several feet is nearly as cold as the water temperature at the bottom. Although it is still warm between the top and the bottom (a thermal column). When this occurs, the fish completely shut down from their normal feeding trends. Generally, as we did that day, you will probably get "skunked".(No Fish!)

The next day we relocated to a Musky lake that had not been getting attention for several years because it was rumoured that it was fished out. This particular body of water had a fair sized river running through it. In my opinion this creates your best conditions for a rehabilitating lake. The river coming in promotes the development of an ideal feeding area for predatory type fish, Musky.

When we arrived at the upper end of the lake, you could envision an imaginary sign saying, "Stop here for some fierce fighting fish!" On the first cast my lure was taken on about the fifth turn of the handle, this metre long Musky literally "kick started" our day. Being a conscientious sport fisherman, it was important to play this fish with some authority, land it quickly and release it unharmed so it could give someone else the same thrill I had been able to experienced.

As the day progressed our next bit of action was another good sized Musky that made a short appearance along side our boat. It seemed uninterested and even less enthusiastic when I performed a "figure eight" with my lure. I guess it was frightened by all the yelling from me and my passengers?

A short time later one of my clients hooked into the "Big Boy" of the day, only to have his lure spit back into his face. My comment to him was, "at least you got to see the Monster"! For our finale the other client managed to catch a late day Musky by rigging a six inch Emerald shiner under a float.

Some other past trips included catching several above average Largemouth Bass caught and released on golf course ponds ten minutes from my back yard. Having the privilege of fishing on a spring fed golf course pond, has to be one of the most exciting ways to fish. Can you imagine, spotting a big Bass, then casting past it, carefully bringing your artificial bait through it's strike zone, then actually watching it gobble up the bait , setting the hook and landing it. One of the best ways to determine how to entice a fish using artificial presentations don't you think!

Late fall also brings a twinkle to my eye when someone asks,"when are you going Salmon fishing? Wrestling Salmon should be an Olympic sport. See Ya out there!!

TROLLING THROUGH THE ICE

For many of us it's the same old standard ice fishing tactics with normal results. Last season I began thinking about how much more effective some of my ice fishing lures might be if I could change the presentation.

Get out the chain saw, cut a hole in the ice about 15 metres long and half a metre wide. Jump on your snow machine and start trolling back and forth. "I don't think so, Tim."

A very effective method that's only been tried me and my friends last season. I call it "the flying jig."

You'll need an ice fishing rod for jigging with an ultra light spinning reel, a package or two of Berkley Power Grubs (3 inch) in white and black metal fleck. You can rig them on 1/4 oz. pink and black round jig heads, with prominent eyes to insure conclusive strikes.

Conventionally you would drop one of these grubs tied directly to the line (no swivel) to the bottom. Then jig up and down constantly until you detect a hit.

Our new method is similar except you drop your bait to the bottom and retrieve it one complete turn of the reel handle. Instead of jigging, you are going to begin by making a slow circular motion directly in front of you about width of a basketball in diameter. As soon as it feels like it is revolving on it's own. Stop! Gently put the rod down beside you so you'll be able to grab it quickly to set the hook.

You'll find that the tip will react very aggressively and harder than a normal strike. What we are doing is teasing or provoking a hit by passing the bait through the fish's strike zone. We are saying, "Na, na, na, na, na —you can't catch me". Seconds later, BANG!, the fish will attack it hard and fast, using the large eye as it's target. With a quick sweeping motion upward, the fight begins. Sounds quite exciting, don't you think?

Also, you can switch from white with a pink head to black with a black head. Determined by what they decide to feed on any given day.

Another option I tried is replacing the grub with a dead minnow by pinching off the head just in front of the gills and installing the

minnows body in the same manner to imitate a minnow fleeing a possible attack.

You will find this technique will produce walleye, perch and pike as well as trout. During the winter fishing season you are allowed to use two rods. One you can leave outside of the hut to give you more room to use method.

Other options are to use Berkley Power Shads (red and black back), or a Mister Twister Silver Shad (3'' black back). To modify your presentation, put your plastic baits into a zip-loc sandwich bag with a tablespoon of sparkle scales gamefish attractant (fish scent) the evening before you plan to go fishing.

If you're an ice hut rental customer, use their tackle and take your own jigging rod set up and terminal tackle as an insurance policy.

If your fishing hole is sixty feet or deeper, increase your jig weight to 3/8 oz. Perch and crappie (calico bass) on the other hand can be caught in the shallows by switching to micro baits. When in doubt, check it out.

THROUGH THICK AND THIN (Fishing Hard Water)

To take the risk out of ice fishing you should learn when to and when not to go out on the ice. It has been my experience that, if you can see through the ice it's probably unsafe to venture on. A rule of thumb is that, four days of well below freezing temperatures should solidify most every body of water. However water depth and motion play an important part of delaying ice freeze-up.

You have probably noticed that ice begins to form from the shoreline out towards the middle of the lake. When the spring thaw starts it's almost the same procedure, except the ice flows are created when edges begin to thaw until the ice mass sinks in the water. Gradually the ice is warmed by the air and moved around by the winds and the rain until it breaks up and eventually melts.

Before heading out on a body of water you should obtain some information about its ice condition. Watching the weather station or listen to a radio weather report is a good practice, so pay close attention to ice hazard warnings.

I have never felt completely confident in driving a vehicle on any frozen lake. Although I may be less inclined to be as nervous if I see several vehicles are already parked in the area to be fished.

As an added precaution, you could simply wear a winterized floatation suit. These suits have been carefully and conscientiously designed for prolonged protection from exposure.

Another tool I have seen but not heard any survival stories about, is the safety devices known as ICESCAPES. They are about six inches long, dowel shaped (rounded wood) about the size of a broom handle. They are worn around your neck and have offset pics to safely fit inside each other. Should you fall through the ice and not panic, you can at least have a chance of climbing out of the water to safety.

In my years of ice fishing I have never actually seem anyone fall through ice or be irresponsible enough to subject themselves to danger.

Have you have ever ventured out to a fishing location where you were not sure of the ice thickness? A good method is listen as you walk, and if you hear squeaking and cracking, retreat. If you don't seem to have a problem continue until you reach your desired spot, cut a hole with your auger and you can see the actual thickness. Some figures that where quoted to me are, (4) four inches is safe for one adult person, (8) eight inches is safe for a snow machine with one person ridding it and (1) one foot is safe for a compact car.

All I can say is PLAY SAFE to avoid self endangerment.

Ice fishing can be a lot of fun if you just use common sense before heading out. Also it's better to over dress for the cold then to not dress for an emergency.

WEB SITES

Use the NET when fishing for information!

- *Master Rod Builder*
  www.dmrods.com
- *Hot Rod Scott's/Thruway Muffler Centre* www.hotrodscotts.com
- *Walleye Fisherman of Ontario*
  www.interlog.com
- *Panther Presentations*
  www.interlog.com
- *Backwood Custom Tackle*
  www.rodblanks.com

"WEBBED SITE"

- *Cover Illustrator and Fine Art Artist* www.trepanieroriginals.com
- *Wishing You were Fishing* www.rodblanks.com
  If you wish to purchase gift copies of this book, call Daniel at: (705) 429-1290 Wasaga Beach.

THE FUTURE OF FISHING...Catch and Release

The New Millennium is upon us, so we will have to work together to maintain or increase the balance of our gamefish population everywhere!

After fishing for nearly half a century it is plain to see that there is a noticeable decline in our fish stocks. The highest percentage of fish are taken for consumption, a lower percent are as a result low mortality rate from careless hook removal and mishandling of fish.

My personal point of view is that the larger species of fish should have reduced take home limit and a minimum size restriction. Rainbow Trout, Salmon, Northern Pike, Muskellunge, Walleye, Bass and Speckled Trout should have a possession limit of one per day. This rule should also apply to tourists as well.

You may have noticed that Bass tournaments throughout North America have been practicing "Catch & Release" for good reason. Although a few fish die, the Bass population in most of these select lakes is still substantial. However the Walleye populations have been suffering dramatically in the last decade due to increased fishing pressure and unreasonably high creel limits. If the limit for Walleye was reduced to three instead of five and a minimum size restriction was enforced we would gain in the probability of reproduction. Most fishing shows advocate the practice of sportfishing as a promising futuristic approach.To reach any level of success the Ministry of Natural Resources should make the necessary limit adjustments as soon as possible and consider restocking public lakes in areas that are suffering from over fishing.

My friends at Advanced Taxidermy have had the right idea for several years now which insure that larger fish (trophies) can be released to fight another day. What they do is Replicate your trophy fish. All they need is a picture, an accurate length measurement and a girth measurement (around the middle of the fish). You don't have to keep the fish! These gentlemen can create an exact replica, masterfully recreated from in-stock moulds then painted with such lifelike appearances that even a fish couldn't tell it wasn't real!

A privately funded group, The Walleye Fisherman of Ontario work with the M.N.R. with a fabulous restocking idea that with the help of private sector contributions and with donations from large corporations will assure that our children will enjoy the "tradition of fishin" in the future. The president of this association, Scott Martin has started the wheels turning and has apparently opened the eyes of many concerned private and business individuals to the obvious need of an Adopt A Walleye Program to brighten our future. A portion of book sales will be donated to support this essential program.

ADOPT A WALLEYE PROGRAM A Chance To Donate For Your Future!

The Walleye Fishermen of Ontario have seen a growing need to protect our walleye fishery for several years. As continued average harvests of walleye remain, we feel natural reproduction of this fish will soon fall short of the yearly harvest. Updated restrictions and continued enforcement, although necessary, do not promote the kind of conservation our group is interested in. We feel the best means of rehabilitating this fragile fishery is by adding to it. By continually stocking walleye, we feel this will sustain the need to set up a put and take relationship that has been a need for some time. The Walleye Fishermen of Ontario are proposing the Adopt A Walleye Program that's sole purpose is to make funds available to the public for the purpose of walleye stocking.

As we are in constant contact with the Ministry of Natural Resources, we will always hear first hand what proposals are upcoming in the area of walleye stocking. Our intent is to then provide access to funds, for the recipient lakes, for the purchase of walleye fry. However, the M. N.R. must ultimately grant approval of whatever stocking is necessary for selected lakes. We can not and will not finance stocking programs without the consent of the M. N. R. In regards to private lakes, The Adopt A Walleye Program will also apply if the intent of the lake owner is to provide access to the general public. We will not subsidize stocking of walleye in lakes with restricted public access. The program is new but very necessary, and with the help of private and public donations could possibly bring about the kind of change this fishery so desperately needs.

ADOPT A WALLEYE FUND

Scott Martin, *President,* The Walleye Fishermen of Ontario
83 Watson Crescent, Brampton, Ontario L6W 1E5
Tel: (416)931-7524 FAX:(905)457-2631
www. interlog. com/ ~ smartin/home.html
Email: smartin@interlog .com

CHAPTER FIVE
Fantastic Freshwater Fish Recipes

Now let's get ready for some good eat'n. It's gonna be a long night. Keep that deck of cards and the church key handy. The morning will be here soon.

COOKING YOUR CATCH...Fish Recipes
(A Testimonial to Dan Sturges from his friend Joe Coniglio)

Catching fish is the most rewarding part of my adventure. While on a trip, I find it equally rewarding to cook and eat our catch. It's the culmination of having fun with family and friends, applied fishing skills and enjoying the good bounty nature provides. The five recipes in Wishing You Were Fishing have been field tested by Dan numerous times and are "tried and true". Beer Batter Walleye is my favorite with its extremely light batter.

Before we met Dan, my father and brothers wanted to get together for dads 80th birthday. Fishing is something we hadn't done collectively in over 25 years! Before the trip, we stood in the garage and looked at all of the old, worn out, mismatched gear and funky tackle. It would have been a total bear to pull it all together, let alone facing the prospects of actually trying to catch fish! We didn't have our own boats either, let alone fishing skills and methods. We were a handful of washed out old bait casters. There were more fish in the lakes and streams then too. Now it takes more skill to catch a fish.

Since we are talking food in this section, Dan did the cooking on our trip–and that was just a small, but important part of what he did! We brought Dan in as our outfitter and guide. I had never met or spoke to him before the trip. We were introduced by Ian Scott of Wishbone Custom Rods. As we got together I was quick to note that Dan had an excellent collection of top notch rods and reels to meet all fishing conditions and specific tackle for bass, walleye and muskies for the lake we were on. He was extremely well organized and family oriented. I don't likely throw the word "pro" around, and Daniel Sturges, (Dan-the-Man) is a consummate Pro! We learned more about fishing in those few days, than in the years of fishing by ourselves. In terms of provisioning, be sure to plan ahead with the proper utensils and ingredients. Oh yeah, Remember the beer batter recipe takes good Canadian beer, which never seems in short supply!

BEER BATTER WALLEYE

2 1/2 lbs. Walleye (or firm fish, like catfish) filleted and skinned
1 1/2 cups buttermilk pancake mix
1 1/2 cups your favourite beer
1 large white or Spanish onion
1/2 lb. small, whole mushrooms
8 large white potatoes, washed and cut

Preheat wok, 2/3 full of canola oil to cook at high heat. Be Careful with kids! Turn all handles inward towards the stove. Cut french fries into New York beefeater size pieces, cook, remove to warming oven set at 200F until ready to serve. Cut fish fillets in two, the tail end just over the halfway mark to make serving sizes similar.

In mixing bowl, add pancake batter and mix with equal amount of beer. Pat dry fillets and dip in coating mix until completely covered. (Six at a time).

Place in the preheated wok, 2/3 full of vegetable oil and cook at high heat.

Turn fish once while cooking so that they brown evenly on sides.

Cook until they float and turn golden brown, (onions, and mushrooms the same way). There's plenty of good beer batter left! dip and coat the sliced onion for onion rings & beer batter fried mushrooms too.

SERVES 8 HEARTY EATERS

GRILLED SALMON STEAKS

4 One Inch Thick Salmon Steaks
1/4 lb Clarified Butter
1 tbsp. Garlic Powder
1 tsp. Fresh Chopped Dill
1 tsp. Cooking oil
1 Lemon, quartered
Salt and Pepper to taste

Preheat barbecue on high heat while you clarify butter. Stir chopped dill into clarified butter and add cooking oil. Brush steak liberally with butter mixture on both sides. Place on heated porcelain grill. Sprinkle on garlic on each steak and flip over. Close barbecue lid for four minutes. Gently turn salmon with a spatula, brush on remaining butter mixture. Close lid and cook for another four minutes. Remove salmon to serving plates and squeeze on juice of lemon wedge.

SERVING SUGGESTION: With steamed vegetables and baked potato with sour cream and dollop of butter. BON APPETITE!

SKILLET FRIED BROOK TROUT

8 Pan Dressed Brook Trout
1 tsp. Heaping, Butter
1/4 tsp. Cooking oil or Bacon fat
1 Cup Bread Crumbs
2 Eggs
1/4 tsp. Garlic Powder

Preheat large frying pan at medium heat. Beat eggs in separate bowl. Dip in beaten egg and tumble through bread crumb mixed with garlic powder. Drop trout in pan, carefully facing thickest end towards centre of pan. Cook for ten minutes or until skin comes off easily and fish flakes when touched with fork. SERVES FOUR

SERVING SUGGESTION: With scrambled eggs and tomato wedges. (This method also works well for smelt & perch)

OVEN BAKED BASS IN TOMATO SAUCE

4 Bass, Pike or Pickerel Fillets
1 Large Can Stewed Tomatoes
1 tbsp. Lemon Juice
8 Sprigs Parsley
1/4 tsp. Garlic Powder
4 tsp. Butter

Preheat oven to 400F. Spray a 9 x 12 pyrex baking dish with non-stick cooking oil. Pat dry fillets and brush lemon on fillets. Add can of stewed tomatoes to baking dish and place fillets in dish. Bake for 20 minutes on lower rack or until fish flakes easily. Lightly dust fillets with garlic powder and place a tablespoon of butter on the middle of each fillet. SERVES SIX
SERVING SUGGESTION: With mashed potatoes, green beans. (MAY SUBSTITUTE LARGE BROOK TROUT, COOKED WITH HEADS REMOVED)

BBQ STUFFED RAINBOW TROUT

1 – 5lb. Rainbow Trout
1 cup Seasoned Croutons
1 Medium Cooking Onion
4 tbsp. Butter
1/4 cup Melted Butter
1 tsp Salt
1 tbsp. Lemon Juice
1 Lemon
Salt and Pepper to taste
1 – 8 oz. can of Emperor Shrimp

Preheat barbecue at high heat. Saturate trout in cold water and place on foil wrap.

Completely fill fish cavity with croutons, the shrimp, half of the onions and butter. Brush cavity with lemon juice. Put one tablespoon of butter at the front and tail end, the same on both sides. Sprinkle salt on dollops of butter. Brush melted butter over exterior of fish. Double wrap trout tightly in foil. Reduce heat to medium and cook fish for 15 to 20 minutes, turning once at half time. SERVES SIX

SERVING SUGGESTION: With partially husked cobs of fresh corn, Caesar salad. Buttered corn can be foil wrapped, placed on the barbecue when fish is half cooked.

ProFishing Guide Services

YOUR HOST PRO FISHING GUIDE
Daniel Sturges

(705)429-1290   GTA FAX (905)896-9675

**49 Acorn Crescent, Wasaga Beach,
Ontario, Canada L0L 2P0
www.rodblanks.com**

Seen frequently on the Ultimate Fishing Show

REPLICATING OPTIONS

I have been fishing for over forty years, I have seen a drastic reduction in game fish populations everywhere. Although the Ministry of Natural Resources has done all they can under the scrutiny of reduced budgets. you may feel as I do, it's time the outdoors enthusiast considers alternatives.

Several years ago I was attending a Spring Fishing Show and there I bumped into two very professional young gentlemen who were promoting fish "replication". Rather than catch and kill your trophy sized fish, you could quickly measure the length and the girth (around the belly measurement), then take a couple of close-up shots with your camera, live release the fish so it could continue to reproduce naturally and may be caught another time or two. By doing this we would increase the fish populations particularly on the heavily fished lakes.

Their idea struck a nerve! Until I met these guys, I had no idea that this process could be done so perfectly, these fellows even enhance the appearance of a natural looking fish. Being interested as I was in art, these two were truly "Masters" at their craft. Not only could these pieces of art grace your walls they could be transformed into pieces of exquisite furniture under glass or executive desk top pen holders. Because you aren't using "skin mounts" there would be no after market maintenance from shrinking.

Next time you catch a big one, remember to bring along a camera and a measuring tape, a piece of paper and a pen, list the measurements, then call **Advanced Taxidermy** and tell them, *Dan sent you!*
